D0061809

"Refreshing and essential for today's Christian parent, *Parenting on Purpose* will make your heart soar! Through vivid anecdotes, honest insights, and wisdom gained in the trenches of raising eight children, Jason Free guides us in all that is crucial to raise our kids Christian — on purpose!"

~ **Donna-Marie Cooper O'Boyle**, Catholic author and
EWTN host of "Everyday Blessings for Catholic Moms"

"What a beautifully written book, filled with wisdom, wit and encouragement for Christian parents! As mother of four and grandmother of five, I learned valuable lessons I can still apply to my own parenting."

~ **Patti Mansfield**, author, conference speaker. www.ccrno.org

"Jason Free's warm, personal, easy-going style is engaging and at the same time challenging. *Parenting on Purpose* made me laugh and cry, but more importantly it made me rethink the way I parent my own children. I am a better dad for having read this book."

~ **Patrick Novecosky**, editor of *Legatus Magazine*; correspondent
for the *National Catholic Register*; contributing writer for
Faith & Family magazine

"Do yourself a favor and spend one short afternoon reading this captivating book. Jason Free first entertains, then provides you with common sense methods to change your child's eternity — on purpose!

~ **Colleen Hammond**, speaker and author of
Dressing with Dignity and *The Gossip's Guide*

"I truly enjoyed *Parenting on Purpose!* With every turn of the page I was boldly affirmed and gently challenged in my own parenthood. This is a great gift for any Christian parent."

~ **Mark Hart**, best-selling Catholic author/speaker;
executive vice president, Life Teen International

"*Parenting on Purpose* can help tilt things back in the right direction for those who take to heart its simple, time-tested, God-centered, common-sense advice on how to effectively 'train up a child in the way he should go.'"

> ~ **Patrick Madrid**, director of the Envoy Institute of Belmont Abbey College; author of *Search and Rescue: How to Bring Your Family and Friends Into (or Back Into) the Catholic Church*

"With *Parenting on Purpose*, Jason Free has offered parents some of that elusive 'magic formula' we're all seeking. Written from the trenches of family life, this book will uplift you, inspire you, and help you to see the blessings inherent in raising faith-filled kids. Kudos!"

> ~ **Lisa M. Hendey**, founder and editor of www.CatholicMom.com; author of *The Handbook for Catholic Moms*

"*Parenting on Purpose* is a must-have guide — fun to read, chock full of practical ideas, and based on solid biblical principles that will keep moms and dads on track through the lifelong adventure of bringing up terrific Christian kids."

> ~ **David Came**, executive editor, *Marian Helper* magazine; author of *Pope Benedict's Divine Mercy Mandate*

"Wow! Finally a book offering practical ways to raise your children as Christians. A first-class spiritual trainer, Jason Free challenges you to decide now what legacy you want to leave to your children."

> ~ **Fr. George W. Kosicki, CSB**, speaker and author of *John Paul II: The Great Mercy Pope*

"This easily read volume blesses us with practical suggestions for prayerful consideration and sound advice for raising a Christian family that is everything God intended it to be. I highly recommend it."

> ~ **Elizabeth Foss**, author of *Small Steps for Catholic Moms* and *Real Learning: Education in the Heart of my Home*

Parenting on Purpose!

7 WAYS TO RAISE TERRIFIC CHRISTIAN KIDS

JASON FREE

Foreword by DANIELLE BEAN

MercySong

STOCKBRIDGE, MASSACHUSETTS

PUBLISHED BY MERCYSONG, INC.
Stockbridge, Massachusetts USA
www.mercysong.com

IN COLLABORATION WITH IGNATIUS PRESS
San Francisco, California, USA

Scripture citations, unless otherwise noted, are taken
from the New American Bible with Revised New Testament,
copyright ©1986, ©1970 by the Confraternity of Christian Doctrine,
Washington, D.C. All rights reserved.

Library of Congress Control No: 2010927575
ISBN-13: 978-1-884479-43-4

"Reflections from Mom" written by Colleen Free

Editorial & Design Direction: Erin Flynn

Cover design by Theodore Schluenderfritz
Interior design by Mary Flannery
Cover Photo by Bounce, Getty Images

PRINTED IN THE UNITED STATES OF AMERICA
October 2010

To Colleen Free
My amazing wife

━━━◦◦━━━

Allow me to join in the chorus with our 8 kids:
You're one terrific mom!

*S*tart a child on the right road, and even in old age he will not leave it."

— PROVERBS 22:6 REB

TABLE OF CONTENTS

Foreword

Years ago, when I was in the hospital laboring to deliver our seventh child, my husband paced the floors, and a television tuned to Fox News blared from a corner of the room.

Pope John Paul II was dying.

It seemed especially fitting that this man, who had spent a lifetime waging battle against the forces of what he called the "culture of death," should offer such a fearless, contrasting example of embracing suffering at the end of his life.

John Paul II was the only pope I ever knew. I was just six years old when white smoke wafted from the chimney in the Sistine Chapel and my mother stood before the television, mesmerized and clutching a dishtowel, as Karol Wojtyla was elected pope decades ago.

Though I paid little attention at the time, the famous opening lines of John Paul II's inaugural sermon came to have more meaning for me as I grew older:

Be not afraid. Open wide the gates to Christ. Open up to his saving power the confines of the state, open up economic and political systems, the vast empires of culture, civilization and development. ... Be not afraid!

It can be hard not to fear.

As parents raising the next generation of Christians in a world that often mocks our values and offers all manner of godlessness presented in seductive packages, it can be very hard not to fear.

That day in the hospital, when my unborn son's heartbeat slowed unexpectedly and became erratic, one nurse ran to the hall and shrieked for the doctor while two others threw me roughly onto my side and forced an oxygen mask onto my face. When my eyes met my pale-faced, stoic husband's, fear pressed hard against my heart.

Hours later, when I held my healthy, pink-faced newborn son, traced my finger along the gentle curve of his dimpled elbows, and felt his sturdy legs kick hard against the swaddling, I thought of our beloved, dying pope. I recalled his abiding love for families and unfailing confidence in the next generation.

John Paul II once said, "As the family goes, so goes the nation and so goes the whole world in which we live."

Sometimes that makes me tremble. We are the families in whom he had such confidence. Ours was the generation he predicted would bring about a "new springtime" in the Catholic Church.

I am no pope. How can I raise up a new generation to wage war against a culture of death that devalues human life, promotes impurity, scorns faith, and forgets its dependence on God?

John Paul II had no patience for such paralyzing fears. I think this is what he had in mind when he reminded us, "The future starts today, not tomorrow." He intended that we should establish a culture of life by forgetting our fears, "opening wide the doors to Christ," and letting Him take care of the more worrisome details.

I am grateful for that reminder.

And Jason Free reminds me too. *Parenting On Purpose* is an easy read, but don't be fooled by its simplicity. Ostensibly, this humble book offers readers "7 Ways to Raise Terrific Christian Kids," but I think what it really offers is something much greater than that. Here, in straight-forward language, with personal examples, practical wisdom, and honest humility, Jason Free offers every Christian parent real hope for the future and an infectious form of optimism.

You can do this, I hear God's voice through these pages. *I have called you to Christian parenthood, and though it might not always be easy, you are up to this task.*

Specifically, Free reminds us to nurture our marriages, bless our children, simplify our lives, celebrate life, speak carefully, protect purity, and create a legacy of love for our families. But the most precious gift in this book is that of parental empowerment. The future of our children's faith is in our hands, but that is not cause for panic. It is cause for great joy. The encouraging, joy-filled chapters of this book will light your heart afire with renewed gratitude for the awesome gift of our faith, and inspire you with confidence as you take on the task of passing on that gift to future generations.

Recently, my son Raphael, born into this world just as John Paul II was leaving it, approached me with a hand-hewn wooden sword his older brother whittled for him from a tree branch.

"Can you attach this to my belt?"

As I worked the sword through his belt loops, Raphael wiped his sun-kissed face with a dirty hand and squinted toward the trees.

"Where can I find some bad guys to fight?" he wondered aloud.

I watched Raphael march boldly into our open field with his sword at his side.

Be not afraid, John Paul II once reminded us, and now Jason Free reminds us too. If we raise up soldiers for Christ, and if we place the future of our Church in such capable hands and hearts as these, we will have nothing to fear.

Danielle Bean
Editorial Director, *Faith & Family*

Hey!
Everything's Different Now!

There's something momentous about the birth of the firstborn. I can remember it as if it were yesterday. … It was just six days before Christmas, and our young, married hearts bubbled over with glee awaiting our eight-pound Christmas present from the stork. The labor and delivery of baby Joseph was a Twilight Zone type of experience for me. Time stood still. I honestly don't think I breathed during the three hours we were in the delivery room. My wife was downright heroic. The whole experience was so sacred and beautiful.

After Joe was weighed and examined thoroughly by the motherly nurses, I was handed the bundled package. My first moments as a father. Gazing at my tiny, swaddled son, I couldn't help but think of what the big day had been like for Mary and Joseph on that star-lit night so long ago.

My tired body melted into the rocking chair. The woman who had given her life to me on the altar — my beautiful bride — now slept peacefully. I never thought I could love her any more, yet a new love was taking root in my heart. A love, I would later learn, that is birthed in parenthood. She was now so much more than a woman and a bride. After giving me another life, she was now a mom. And I a dad.

The gray December sky littered the countryside with snow. Yet the spirit of spring was in my heart. In an instant, a new life had sprouted into the cold world. And I held him.

Everything is different now. "Where did that thought come from?" I wondered. Was it whispered into my ear by my guardian angel? Or was I just realizing the immensity of this miraculous event?

I guess the source of those musings was really irrelevant. I knew that those four simple words revealed a profound truth. Everything is different now. If my wife and I were holding on to any last vestiges of adolescence, the thread had been cut. With one quick intake of air, our son had catapulted us into a life of sacrifice, hardship, and joy that can only be found in the great adventure called parenthood.

I knew that just doing whatever we wanted to do was now gone. Sleeping in would be a distant memory. She and I were turning the page and getting ready to write a whole new chapter. Actually, forget that — more like writing a whole new book. Our little family would now be engrossed in car seats, diaper rash, and putrid-colored baby food. Sleep deprivation would be similar to what the Navy Seals undergo in their rigorous boot camp training. Soon, I pondered, he'll be watching Sesame Street on PBS, then he'll be playing Little League, and before we know it he'll need braces. At this point, I pictured my son growing at a rate triple that of the weeds in my garden. My heart raced. Heck, before I know it, he'll be taking his driving test and heading off to college. … "Slow down, Jay," I said to myself in a reassuring tone. "It'll be OK. One day at a time."

"Yeah, everything is different now," I said with fear and trembling. Ready or not, I was now a dad. I'm sure I'm not the first guy who frantically looked around the maternity ward for the *How To Raise a Terrific Christian Kid* instruction manual, am I? Instead, all we got when we left the hospital was a free diaper bag and a sweet congratulatory smile from the head nurse as she closed our car door.

We were off. Nervous, excited, and oh so green. I desperately hoped my voice would make it through the heavy snowflakes that came from above as I prayed, "Please God … help us to have what it takes to be great parents."

Seven children later, I'm still offering that prayer to heaven. And just so you know, every time my lovely bride brought forth new life from her womb, I also found myself speaking the profoundly simple phrase that seemed to capture the significance of the moment: *Everything's different now.*

After our third baby, or maybe it was the fourth (one of the effects of prolonged parental sleep deprivation is memory loss), I stopped looking for the instruction manual. By this point, the mother of all learning (trial and error) had given us a crash course.

I would be completely arrogant and flat-out wrong to even remotely suggest that you have in your hands a bona fide Christian parenting instruction manual. There are no PhDs hanging above my fireplace. I'm no child-development guru. I am just a forty-year-old dad who's madly in love with his kids and wants them to know just how madly in love God is with each of them.

Even though we didn't always have a clue, one thing I can say with certainty is this: My wife and I always wanted to raise terrific Christian kids — on purpose. If you're holding this book, I imagine the same is true for you. I hope that our stories, techniques, and reflections will be one huge blessing for your home.

May the God who "makes all things new" pour His grace into your heart and provide you with a vision of how to love and raise your children. "Everything is different" once you become a parent, but remember: Our Father's love for you and your kids never changes. It is the same yesterday, today, and forever.

Be Madly in Love with Your Spouse And Let Your Kids See it!

otcha! Here we are on the first chapter, and you're undoubtedly ready to sink your teeth into a juicy tip that would be perfect for your son's or daughter's Christian upbringing. A strategy never thought of before by man that would direct your children's sights onto Jesus and fill them with a love that would bring tears to your eyes. Don't worry, we'll get there. But remember, you can't get the car out of the garage unless you put that ol' key in the ignition. There's no getting to first base without stepping into the batter's box. I think you get the point.

In the very core of every child's heart there is a longing that we seldom talk about. It's not what most think. He isn't yearning for the latest game system, a $200 Little League bat, a skateboard, or a pony. No, from the time of his first breath, his soul has been longing to be united with the love that continuously flows from the Trinity. This might be hard for you to swallow, but he is really longing to be home in the loving embrace of his Father. We all are, for that matter.

> As a deer longs for streams of water,
> so my soul longs for you, O God.
> My being thirsts for God, the living God.
> When can I go and see the face of God?
>
> PSALM 42:1-2

But kids don't know this. Heck, most of us adults forget that our true destination is heaven — the place where perfect love resides. We get caught up in rushing Johnny to his travel soccer game and little Susie to her horseback riding lessons. Moms and dads have become mired in a world of organized sports, extracurricular activities, and the perfect Disney vacation.

So let's get back to the basics. Ready? Hold on tight, 'cause this is a biggie. Your child's first glimpse of the love to be found in heaven is *your marriage*. How else will her little mind grasp the love that flows between the Father, Son, and Holy Spirit except by observing the love that flows between mom and dad? The pure love between the

Father and the Son is so real that it's actually another person — the Holy Spirit. In matrimonial love, the man and woman give themselves to one another, and the fruit of that sacred love is the birth of a whole new person.

As parents, there are many strategies we can implement to foster our children's relationship with the Savior. I got news for ya — that's the easy part. In later chapters we'll hit on some of those concrete ideas. But ideally, every Christian parenting technique must flow from a relationship of love expressed between Mom and Dad. Your child longs for this; he hungers to see his parents in love.

Too often, parents get lost in jobs, bills, kids' activities, and lawns that just gotta be mowed. I know. I've been there. Before you can blink, years have passed, hairlines have receded, and, sadly, love has sometimes faded. Each day, Junior observes. His eyes are locked onto your marriage. He's longing to see Dad come home from work with flowers and a passionate kiss for Mom. He may shout in disgust at the display of affection, but his soul shouts for joy.

I distinctly remember my mom and dad going on dates. My mom would talk about wanting to "make herself beautiful" as she brushed eyeliner around her soft, green eyes. My nine-year-old nose told me she smelled pretty as she sprayed on her perfume. I loved seeing my mom wrap her arms around Dad's neck when he came home with fresh-cut flowers for her. They kissed. And then they were off to dinner. You know how I felt at that moment? Whole. Secure. At home. Sound like heaven?

You wanna raise terrific Christian kids? You really want them to understand God's love? Then the first and foremost thing you can do is have a great marriage. Love your spouse, and for God's sake — let your kids see it!

Let's roll up our sleeves...

All right, time to get practical.
To wrap up each chapter, we'll hit on three key steps that will help you raise outstanding Christian kids.

TAKE STOCK. On a scale of one to ten (one being "pathetic" and ten being "as good as the Trinity"), observe just how well you and your spouse show love to one another in front of the kids. Don't breeze by this first step. A doctor can't prescribe a treatment unless he's aware of the severity of the ailment. Your marriage has got to take precedence over the electric bill and a manicured front lawn. Take some quiet time with your spouse and honestly evaluate your love score. Remind yourself that you'll be a much happier person if your love grows. Your kids' faith is depending on it!

"My Love Score"
1..2..3..4..5..6..7..8..9..10
(10 being the highest-possible grade)
Grade yourself on how well you and your spouse express love in front of the kids.
Now ask the kids to grade you.

A word of caution here — and this is coming from someone who taught marriage counseling in graduate school — once you give yourself a grade, don't freak out on me. Please! Remember, discouragement ain't a virtue. Recognize that things could be better, and move on.

TAKE ACTION. Go out on a date! It can't get any more basic than this. Don't just make a vague resolution to spend more time with one another, but commit to a "date night" at least once every two weeks. This sends a powerful message to your kids:

Hey guys, Mom and Dad really love each other, and we have to have some alone time. We love you and everything, but this is our time.

You know that you have fully committed to a date night if you can verify it on your calendar. There's nothing wrong with spontaneously grabbing a bite to eat, but let's face it, the older the kids get, the less free time we have to play around with. If it's really important, you'll schedule it. Otherwise, it's more than likely that it won't happen.

Trust me — I know.

Don't think you have to go crazy here. No need to rent a tux and re-mortgage the house for a fancy dinner. Be creative. Go miniature golfing, have a picnic, or find a restaurant with an early bird discount. I'd highly recommend you not hide behind a movie screen where you watch other people loving one another. Do something where you actually interact. *Schedule this date night in advance and stick to it!*

TAKE TIME TO PRAY. As the famous saying goes, we saved the best for last. You really want your love for your spouse to grow? Like *really*? Then no amount of date nights can compare with praying together for fifteen minutes each day. If we took a poll on the number of Christian spouses who actually pray together, consistently, we'd be aghast. We have twenty-four hours in a day, yet somehow our day planners and smartphones can't help us squeeze in fifteen minutes for Mom and Dad to spend together in prayer. What's with that?

I know, I know, I've heard the excuses. Heck, I've said 'em: *I'm getting pulled in a million directions. The demands of the job keep growing, and my boss is all over me. Kids need to be taxied to this activity and the next. The pile of bills has become a mountain. Blah, blah, blah, blah, blah.* So what? All the more reason to take a little time and ask the God of the universe for some help.

Don't get overwhelmed with this last step. I'm not asking you to rise at 2 a.m. with the monks. Just light a candle. Hold your spouse's hand. Pick a Scripture

ROLL UP YOUR SLEEVES RESOURCES

- *The 5 Love Languages,* by Dr. Gary Chapman
- *Weekend to Remember Marriage Conference,* hosted by FamilyLife.com

passage and read it. Thank the Father for your marriage, the leftovers in the fridge, and your kid's beating heart. Then ask Him for help with those bills and the cantankerous boss. Tell your spouse that you want to love her more, and ask God to bless this most worthy goal. (He will!) Pray the Lord's Prayer. Slowly. And mean it. Amen.

There, that wasn't too bad. Fifteen minutes and you're a new you. Fifteen minutes spent like this, day in and day out, will also make your child a better Christian, especially if she sees that you make prayer a top priority.

One last thought on prayer. There's nothing wrong with praying by yourself and spending some one-on-one time with the Almighty. We all need more of that. But remember, if you want a great marriage, there's no substitute for praying with the person you said those vows to.

I dare you and your spouse to take the fifteen-minute challenge: For thirty straight days, the two of you pray with one another for just 900 seconds. (That equals fifteen minutes for all you non-math types out there.) That doesn't seem too hard, does it? What do you think? Will you do it? Or just read about doing it?

Be sure to let your kids see you praying together. God willing, they'll grow up and marry someone whom they can pray with, too. What Christian parents wouldn't want that for their children?

Reflections from Dad . . .

I specifically remember the first time Colleen and I prayed together as a married couple. We had settled into our two-bedroom, $330 per month, second-story apartment. We were broke. Actually, a little beyond that — our wedding money was paying for groceries and the electric bill. I was finishing up my master's degree in a full-time, unpaid internship. Colleen was having a hard time landing a teaching job. All in all, our marriage wasn't off to a prosperous start, and we were a tad stressed.

Our extra bedroom made for a perfect place to pray. I placed a religious cassette tape in the deck and flipped open the Bible. Colleen read: "Therefore I tell you, do not be anxious about your life, what you shall eat or what you shall drink ... Look at the birds of the air: they neither sow nor reap nor gather into barns, and yet your heavenly Father feeds them. Are you not of more value than they?"
Matthew 6:25-26 (RSV)

In an instant, the Word of God slammed my

financial fears to the ground. It was in the intimacy of praying with my spouse that I — no, scratch that —WE were able to ask God for help and peace. I realized early on in my marriage that talking about the stresses of life is one thing, but praying about them with my wife — that's the real thing!

Reflections from Mom...

After a crazy day of being with the kids, I got the call every wife dreams of: Jay was picking up pizza for the kids, and he asked if I'd like to go out for dinner. As if I was going to refuse the chance to eat without having to clean up spilled milk or cut someone else's meat! And we might even get the chance to have an uninterrupted conversation!

Unfortunately, it was tourist season in our New England town, and every restaurant had a forty-five-minute wait. I knew that my Type A husband was not about to wait that long. "Why don't we just go grab some subs and enjoy the nice weather?" I suggested.

In no time we were having a beautiful summer picnic. We prayed, ate our simple meal, and relished our alone time in the July sun. It brought me right back to our first dates seventeen years ago, when we were young, broke, and totally in love. The dates I remember best were spent just like this one.

CHAPTER 2

Teach Blessing

I couldn't help but venture into the online dictionary to see what the really smart people have to say about the biblical word "bless." Here you go: 1) "To hallow or consecrate by religious rite or word;" 2) "to hallow with the sign of the cross;" 3) "to invoke divine care for;" 4) "to confer prosperity or happiness upon."

It's a fascinating word. Grammatically gifted folks like my wife, Colleen, are quick to point out that "bless" is a transitive verb. Folks like me, who have an unhealthy dependence on editors, can only tell you it's a darn good word. And one that's essential to embrace if you truly want to raise terrific Christian kids.

From the very beginning of His public ministry, the thirty-three-year-old carpenter from Galilee set out to bless His people. In fact, one could surmise that His very life, death, and resurrection were nothing more than one mammoth heavenly blessing from above.

Remember the time He extended His hand to the adulterous woman whose face lay in the earth just waiting for the first stone to hit? She was demoralized. Caught in sin. And viciously ridiculed by the public. Yet Jesus intervened and offered forgiveness, a second chance. Sounds like blessing par excellence.

There are so many biblical instances where Jesus "invoked divine care for" sinners, prostitutes, beggars, and tax collectors. But that was more than two thousand years ago. What about now? What about in your home?

Your home and mine must be defined as places of blessing. This is paramount. If Jesus came to bless and we're His followers, I guess it makes sense that we follow His lead. Keeping it practical, you don't have to sell your home and cash in your 401k to live out your faith. The home provides the perfect place to bless up a storm.

Do you know why we say "God bless you" to someone who just kachooed? Why would a spontaneous sneeze from a pollen-laden allergy sufferer invoke such an act of piety? I've heard that it's because folks used to believe that when you sneeze, your heart actually stops beating. This "nasal blessing" actually had a purpose — to keep your life going! It was a type of heavenly defibrillator, if you will.

When Colleen was pregnant with our first child, her

dad gave us a book that talked about a fascinating concept — praying for your unborn child. It was a great read and a real eye-opener. And such a blessing. The author eloquently conveyed that our child, who was two months old at that time and enjoying the aquatic life of the womb, could sense our love for him. This would continue for the whole nine months and only grow in intensity. The conclusion, of course, was that we could have a significant impact on this developing life by verbally blessing our baby every day.

In earnest, we began this prenatal laying on of hands. I would speak to our son as Colleen's hand rested on mine: "Joe, it's Dad. I'm so glad you're my son. We can't wait to hold you and love you. I ask God to bless you with all the grace in heaven. And I bless you, Joe." This ritual would go on month after month until it was showtime. I still remember the look on Colleen's face when we rushed with great, early-morning panic and excitement to the maternity ward.

As I held this twenty-two-inch young life for the first time, I was overjoyed to finally see the baby we had been praying for during the course of the pregnancy. He smiled at me, and it was now my turn to be blessed. For nine months, I had prayed over his mother's growing stomach, and now I felt enveloped in the Father's divine care as I looked upon this amazing new life. But the blessings didn't stop there. They never do. God's blessings just have a way of multiplying and overflowing.

Colleen rested after her heroic performance, and the nurse was taking a lunch break. Joe and I were alone. He rested peacefully in my arms. All of heaven looked on as I did what seemed right at the time — I blessed him. *Lord, thank you for this beautiful life. You allow his heart to beat. You've blessed our marriage with this boy. I claim him for You, God. I ask you to bless him here on day one, Lord. And Joe, little buddy, I bless you.* Joe opened his eyes and offered an approving smile. My wife later told me that he probably just had gas, but I didn't believe it for a minute!

As our little man grew into his ever-so-enjoyable terrible two's, the habit of blessing was fully rooted in our family life. It was just as much a part of the nighttime ritual as brushing teeth, going potty, and reading a story. As he lay there with the soft glow of the night light on his face, Colleen or I would place a hand on his forehead and bless him. This was his last experience of us every night before he drifted off to sleep.

I'll never forget the cold, winter night when it clicked in Joe's young mind that he, too, could invoke divine care by offering a blessing. I had blessed him for the night and had turned to leave, when it appeared he was trying to slap my glasses. Not wanting his fingerprints all over them, I pulled away and urged him to stop. "Don't hit Daddy," I said in a stern tone. But he kept on.

"I bwess Daddy," he joyfully exclaimed, reaching again for my forehead. For the first time, Joe began to do what our Lord started so many years ago.

"How about that!" I exclaimed. I honestly hadn't thought about teaching him how to bless. "You're on to something, Joe," I encouraged as I tousled his hair. "Who said that only adults can bless? Good job, my little man. From now on, Daddy has to get your blessing, too." He giggled in excitement as I left his room. "Hey, Hon," I proudly called out to my wife, who was nursing the baby. "Our Christian kid just started acting like a Christian!"

Let's roll up our sleeves...

TAKE STOCK. How much blessing goes on in your house? This area must be of great concern for every household. If you dare, ponder the counterfeits of blessing: sarcasm, shaming, cutting words, and the silent treatment. Ouch! We've all been the recipients of those bad boys and certainly know the emotional and spiritual price we paid. If yours is like most households in America, no doubt there's a whole lot more blessing that could be going on. Become aware of the Father's desire to bless your life — seek it. Open your heart to the blessings God wants to lavish on you. After all, you're His kid!

Take the "Blessing" pop quiz:

1. In the last seven days, have you placed your hand on your child's head and blessed her? ☐ Yes or ☐ No

2. In the last seven days have you consciously spoken encouraging words to your son? Affirmed him not just for getting a good grade or hitting the ball into left field, but JUST BECAUSE he's your son and his life gives you joy? ☐ Yes or ☐ No

3. Is "God Bless You" reserved for sneezing only? ☐ Yes or ☐ No

TAKE ACTION. Whether you've been praying for your kids since the moment of conception or not, today is a new day. It's never too late to start blessing, but it takes a strong decision to make it a habit. That's the goal here. Commit to graduating from the "sneeze blessing" to blessing your child on purpose.

❖ Start with bedtime.

❖ How about when your daughter leaves the house for school or a sleepover?

❖ When your son is anxious about the Little League game, don't stop with advice on having a good "at bat." Throw that young Babe Ruth on your lap and bless him. Tell him that no matter what, he's a champion because he's God's awesome creation.

ROLL UP YOUR SLEEVES RESOURCES

- *The Healing Power of a Father's Blessing,* by Linda Schubert
- *Praying for your Unborn Child,* by Francis & Judith MacNutt
- *Will You Bless Me?,* by Neal Lozano

❖ When you're anointing that skinned knee with antibacterial cream, how about slapping on a blessing, too?

Here's the point. Blessings are not reserved for big events like weddings and Thanksgiving dinner. They're for all year round. You don't need a theological degree from Harvard to spot all the opportunities to invoke divine care on your child in the ordinariness of life. Just do it!

TAKE TIME TO PRAY. The blessing is really meant to be spoken. Don't get me wrong; there's nothing spiritually improper about praying for someone in the quiet of your heart. But verbally invoking God's favor and divine care on your child can never be underestimated. It's powerful, life-changing, and easy. Here's a quick walk-through:

1. Place your hand on your daughter's head.

2. In a voice that she can hear, thank God for her life. *Oh, Lord, I thank you so much for Maggie. I love her life, and I praise you for keeping her healthy today.*

3. Then thank Him for the blessing it is to be her parent. Express the gratitude you have for the privilege of having this child.
   I am so blessed to have her in my life. Maggie, I love being your Dad.

4. Now speak a blessing over your daughter. And I mean this literally. Something like: *I love you so much, Maggie, and as your Dad, I ask our faithful God in heaven to bless every cell in your body. And I bless you. Goodnight, sweetheart.*

No Orlando timeshare, designer Nike sneakers, or iPod could ever impact your child more than this simple ritual.

Reflections from Dad...

When my job was sending me overseas for ten days, I found myself in a quandary, because I had really been enjoying the routine of reading to the kids and blessing them at bedtime. I also enjoyed their little hands fumbling through my receding hairline as I received their blessing. So my wife and I came up with an idea: We grabbed the video camcorder, and for every night I was going to be away, she recorded me reading a bedtime story. Upon completion of the story, I would look directly into the camera, extend my hand toward the camera lens, and bless each child by name. Colleen told me that the kids loved to watch the video while I was away.

Fast-forward to present day: My teenage son recently stumbled upon this video. He placed it into the VCR and instantly remembered the stories and blessings he had received by video when he was only four. Trust me on this — your kids will never forget being blessed by you.

Reflections from Mom...

I didn't truly realize the impact that our "blessings" were having on our kids until one fateful afternoon in the backyard. Maggie, about three at the time, and Johnny, one and a half, were chasing each other around and shrieking in delight as only toddlers can do.

As I watched from the deck, I saw Johnny suddenly trip and face plant into the grass. The shrieking was no longer delightful! Maggie reached him first, and I looked on in amazement as she helped him to his feet, gave him a hug, and placed her chubby little hand on his head with the sweetest "God bless Johnny" I had ever heard. Music to a mother's ears!

CHAPTER 3

Sometimes Less is More

The Swartzentruber Amish are known to be the most conservative of the dozen or so Amish churches throughout America. No electricity. That means no air conditioning on thick, humid July days. No forty-eight-inch plasma flat-screen to catch the Notre Dame football game on Saturday. Forget designer clothes like Polo and L.L. Bean — these folks even forgo elaborate trimmings like zippers. Plain, black, horse-drawn buggies are the transportation of choice, regardless of the time of year. Schedules are rigid, and faith takes the highest of priorities for these large families, who appear to us modern folk as being stuck in the days of *Little House on the Prairie.*

Cuff-linked New York City marketers have made a mint on these simple folk. Movies, calendars, figurines, cookbooks, and romance novels have cashed in on our fascination with this population that seems to be lost in time.

What is it that captivates us so? Why do bus tours by the dozens make their way through the pristine country roads of Lancaster County, Pa.? What are the passengers hoping to see? A barefoot Amish boy running through a watermelon patch? Or perhaps a young Amish couple taking a buggy ride on a quiet Sunday afternoon? Maybe the attraction we often feel toward our Amish brethren is speaking to a deeper longing we're not fully aware of.

By now, you're probably getting ready for me to bring out the big guns and lead you down a path that bemoans the evils of modernization, technology, and all things material. However, as I sip my Starbucks latte, I know that would be all too hypocritical. Don't worry, I'm not going to hurl some Scripture verse at you where you hear Jesus instructing His newly found disciple to "go and sell all that you have" before following Him.

Nope. My wife keeps reminding me that "extremes" of anything are often, well, *extreme*. I would argue for a moment, however, that the typical Christian kid today is involved in a war that you may not know about. It's the battle for Christian simplicity.

Let me illustrate my point. My oldest son, Joe, approached me in earnest one afternoon and said that he needed to speak with me. "Yeah, Joe, what's up?" I asked, turning from my laptop.

"Dad," he began, "I know that we're getting ready for our family trip, and I was thinking ... ah, hold on a minute," he said, distracted by his cell phone. It was a text message from his friend. Apparently, there was an emergency. This teenage texter had a question about advancing to the next level on his Xbox video game.

Annoyed with this disturbance, I pushed him on. I didn't have a lot of time to waste. After all, there was useless e-mail to gaze at. "Yeah, and ..." I said with exaggeration.

"Well, Dad, it's a long trip. Like eight hours or something. And I was thinking that we should try to get one of those portable DVD players for the ride. For the kids, you know?" he said with a serious look.

"Mmm. For the kids," I said with a twinge of sarcasm. "OK, let me think about it ... no."

"What are we gonna do then?"

"You know what we can do in the car, Joe? What your grandparents did before the dawn of cell phones, laptops, DVD players, and hand-held electronic games. We'll talk to one another. Mom will probably bring some books and read aloud. We'll play 'I Spy' and license-plate bingo. In those eight hours, I bet we'll manage to find some time to pray. As a family. Oh, and you know those clear, glass things on the side of the car?"

"Duh ... windows, you mean?" he replied as only a teenager can.

"Yeah, those things," I went on. "We'll look out of 'em and see the world instead of staring zombie-eyed at an artificial one." Joe walked away in defeat, and I sang a triumphant song for simplicity's sake.

This true example is no stretch, is it? Kids today are enticed by video games that seem to have more detail and clarity than real life. I remember playing "Pong" on my Atari games system. I controlled a block that had to hit a square, bouncing techno ball. Now kids are so virtual, I wonder how many of them have even held a real ball in their hands.

iPods, game systems, smartphones, Facebook, texting, Twittering, and two hundred channels on cable ... how much more do we need? I remember participating in a college philosophy course where my professor intelligently stated that technology had one purpose — to improve the quality of life. I thought he was so smart, and I think he did as well, as he looked at us through his John Lennon spectacles. His tweed jacket was perfect for the setting. "So, class, has it?" he mused.

But let's get back to the Amish. Perhaps we are mesmerized by them because they offer us a reminder of what life used to be like in simpler days. Big families in small houses. Wearing our "Sunday best" to church. Books, rag dolls, board games, fishing holes, and hopscotch were the norm. Children would play outside for hours, unattended. Houses were built with front porches so we could leisurely swing and sip Grandma's lemonade before a big, home-made, Sunday afternoon dinner.

Now it's organized play dates, $100 American Girl dolls, virtual fishing games, and food that's been processed to the hilt and zapped in the microwave as we sit in front of our high-definition TV. Sunday, once a day of leisure (remember most stores used to be closed?), has now been replaced as the day of choice for kids' sporting events.

I'm telling ya, there's a war going on that most Christians don't even know they should be fighting. This technological foe rages on, without need for rest, and it seeks to overwhelm your child with activities that waste time and can be harmful to your child's soul.

Terrific Christian kids need a hearty dose of simplicity in their lives. Sometimes less really is more. Read that sentence again. Go on, it's true. I'll never forget the time my wife and I decided to "kill the TV." We were tired of frantically changing channels when sex-laden commercials popped on the idiot box or explaining to our kids why a popular sitcom really wasn't that cool.

"Let's just get rid of it," Colleen proposed.

"Yeah, let's go Amish!" I chimed in, dialing the cable company on my cell phone. We were both more than ready to cut the electronic umbilical cord we had been attached to.

It took a while for the family to get accustomed to the loss of our friend. We went through the typical stages of grief. First there was shock and anger: *What?! No more Disney Channel, Dad? What about watching football on Sundays?* Admittedly, I went through severe shakes with *Sports Center* withdrawal. Then came the rationalization phase: *C'mon, Dad, we could be learning from the Discovery and History channels. And then the desperation phase: I'm sure there are some good shows on the Christian channel that we're missing, Dad.*

"Sorry," I replied over and over again. "We've gone Amish on this one."

Suddenly something remarkable happened. Out came the board games and Uno cards. Some of the kids actually wanted to learn chess! Library cards were renewed. In no time, the gentle gal behind the library desk knew all our kids' first names. Dust was blown off the coloring books. The back yard was transformed into a playfield for games like hide-n-seek, tag, and wiffleball. We noticed an immediate increase in snow forts, splinters, skinned knees, and sunburned faces. It was awesome!

Above and beyond the paring down of the techno-craze, family prayer became more prevalent. Not a bad thing, huh? By shedding some of the "stuff" that was making us so terribly busy, we actually were able to find more time for God. Simplicity had won a victory in our home, and in multiple ways our children were the better for it.

Let's roll up our sleeves...

TAKE STOCK. It'd be foolish to cover the topic of Christian simplicity without talking about priorities and basic time management. Spend a few minutes honestly answering the following questions:

❖ On an average weekend, how many minutes/ hours do you spend in front of the computer?

_____

❖ On an average weekend, how many minutes/ hours do you spend in front of the TV?

_____

❖ On an average weekend, how many minutes/ hours do you spend with your kids?

_____

❖ On an average weekend, how many minutes/ hours do you spend praying with your kids?

_____

Now, that you're done, ask someone who has the opportunity to observe you on a day-to-day basis to assess you.

Time management and priority management should be mandatory courses for high school graduation. Kids today are suffering from sensory overload. Hours upon hours are spent on Facebook, the cell phone, or the hottest $50 video game. The deception is that since they were so "busy," they actually think they were doing something productive. And, let's face it; adults are often just as guilty of it.

Listen, stop saying: *I don't have the time*, or *I'm so busy*. News flash: All you really have is time. After waking up you have, on average, about sixteen hours before you hit the sack. So spend those precious 960 waking minutes wisely. Don't get caught up in the allures of the world. Put your foot down. Simplify. Your kids are watching you, needing your backup in this battle for Christian simplicity.

TAKE ACTION. This is the fun part! Once the scales fall from the eyes and you unleash your creative mind, there's no limit to living simply.

Here's a start:

❖ **Limit TV time.** Or, if you want to launch a full assault, kill the TV!

❖ **Grab the picnic basket and traipse off to the nearest state park.** Go on a leisurely hike and drink in the wonders of God's artistic hand.

❖ **Introduce fasting to your home.** If you want to raise terrific Christian kids, this is guaranteed to build spiritual muscle. Contrary to popular opinion, fasting isn't reserved for those who hung out with the likes of Moses. Christian simplicity demands that we know how to deny ourselves. Self-control is a virtue. Start slow. Perhaps one night a week dinner is confined to a bowl of soup and some homemade bread. Or make Sundays "family treat day," whereas during the week you "just say no" to Twinkies, Coca-Cola, and gummy bears. Our fast-food nation won't understand, but your son's soul will flourish and mature as he learns to simplify and hunger for the things of heaven.

> ### ROLL UP YOUR SLEEVES RESOURCES
>
> - *The Simple Life*, by Wanda E. Brunstetter
> - *100 Ways to Simplify Your Life*, by Joyce Meyer
> - *Continual Feast*, by Evelyn Vitz

❖ **Have an "Amish night."** I'm serious. Get the whole family involved in making a homemade dinner. The microwave is off limits! Eat by candlelight. Make it a technology-free home from dinner to bedtime. No phone calls, texting, or computer. Have fun with this one — you'll be amazed at how much your kids get into it. And how much you get into it!

❖ **Read to your kids.** There's nothing like sitting next to your mom and hearing her voice as she walks with you through the adventures of books. This time can also be spent reading about the heroic lives of the saints. Before Superman, these were the first action heroes.

TAKE TIME TO PRAY. The battle for time well spent and priorities managed properly can only be won in prayer. Here is where Christian simplicity is continuously renewed. First and foremost, prayer with your spouse must be the norm, not the exception. Remember, the typical American couple has sixteen waking hours at its disposal. Make time to pray about your marriage, family life, and child's soul.

Secondly, if life becomes too busy to fit in family prayer, then it's time to call for heavenly backup. This just can't be. Not if you desire to raise a terrific kid who knows and loves the Lord.

Prayer time in the home doesn't have to be complicated. A few thoughts on keeping it simple:

❖ **Make it a habit.** You get up at the same time every day. You eat dinner at the same time. How about lifting your hearts to God at the same time every day? I know there will be exceptions, but you get the point. Whether it's 7 a.m. or 7 p.m., write your family prayer time into the daily routine.

❖ **Make it fresh.** Mix up the way you pray. Don't be so rigid. Here are some ideas plucked right out of Scripture.

The following verses are from Colossians 3:15-17:

And be thankful (VERSE 15).

- How about focusing some prayer time expressing thanks to God for all the ways your family has been blessed. See how many times you can thank Him. There's so much to be thankful for — so do it!

Let the word of Christ dwell in you richly
(VERSE 16).

- Perhaps one day you and your child pick a Scripture passage and read it. Slowly. Then spend ten minutes talking about it.

*Sing psalms and hymns and spiritual songs
with gratitude in your hearts to God
(VERSE 16).*

- Nothing lifts the soul like praising God in song. Devote one night of family prayer to singing praise and worship songs. If you're musically challenged like me, put in a religious CD, turn up the volume, and sing from your heart.

❖ **Make it personal.** This is huge. If you want to raise a terrific Christian kid, then helping him have a personal relationship with Jesus is vital. Remember, He's counted every hair on your head. He knows what you do every waking moment. Just going through the motions for the sake of praying doesn't cut it. Like a potato chip, there's no value in it. Teach your child to pray about the cares on his heart. As my wise teenage son often says, "Keep it real."

The Colossians Scripture passage I referenced ends with a powerful sentence. It poignantly reminds us exactly what we need to do to maintain a spirit of Christian simplicity and nurture that same spirit in our kids as well. Care to pray it with me?

And whatever you do, in word or deed,
do EVERYTHING in the name of the Lord Jesus
(VERSE 17).

Amen.

Reflections from Dad...

I'll never forget the summer I almost chose to miss out on my son's Cub Scout camp. The demands of work were high, and I was feeling pulled in a million directions. "I'm just so busy," I whined to my wife as I brought up the possibility of skipping out on camp.

Listen, I don't want to underestimate the pressures involved in being a parent. Mortgage payments, bills, braces ... it's a lot, I know. But if you want to raise a terrific Christian kid, you've got to spend time with him. No fancy gadgets or expensive vacations can serve as a substitute for time.

"You're not here on this earth to pay the electric bill, Jay," she said truthfully. "Before you know it, Johnny won't be going to Cub Scout camp; he'll be off to college and starting a life of his own."

I knew that I couldn't miss out on a chance to just be with him. In this hectic day and age, those opportunities happen all too infrequently. So I packed my duffle bag, grabbed my hiking stick, and shared a tent with my son for six holy days.

We did everything a boy loves to do: shot BB guns, canoed around the lake, made fires, and sang songs in the mess hall. We even set aside some quiet time to pray. Just the two of us. Father and son, away from the world, reading God's sacred Word on a crystal-clear August day. It was perfect.

On our last day at camp, Johnny and I were walking along a trail reflecting on the fun week we had had. "We only have a few hours left, Johnny," I said. "What should we do? Go to archery? How about the camp store for a Snickers bar? This is your time, son. What d'ya say?"

He placed his hand in mine. I silently wondered how much longer he'd want to hold his dad's hand. Soon, his teenage friends would let him know that it wasn't cool. I relished the moment. I wouldn't have traded that walk on the trail for a winning lottery ticket that paid all my electric bills for life.

Johnny squeezed my hand and smiled at me. "I just want to be with you, Dad. I don't care what we do. Thanks for coming to camp with me. You're the best."

My spirit soared. Another small victory won in the battle for Christian simplicity.

Reflections from Mom...

I have a confession to make: I'm an "eBay-aholic."

It all started innocently enough. As a stay-at-home, homeschooling mother of eight, I was in the habit of trying to save money wherever I could, so I thought I'd check out this "eBay thing" I'd been hearing about to see if I could get some cheap schoolbooks.

I didn't realize how time-consuming this would be. I did save hundreds of dollars, but I spent hours upon hours searching, and then bidding and checking to see if I'd won each auction. I got some great deals, but that was my Achilles' heel. I've always had a hard time passing up a good deal. Before I knew it, I was hooked. And I was able to rationalize it because I was "saving money for the family."

I began looking for all sorts of things: strollers, baby clothes, maternity clothes, Christmas gifts. I knew it was becoming an issue when I would quickly shut it off as I heard Jason come in from work so he wouldn't know I was on the computer.

Little by little, the Lord began to convict me of my sin: I had made an idol of eBay! Not only that, but I was also showing my kids how to walk down the same road.

One day, my daughter Maggie asked me if she could play a computer game. I told her I didn't want her spending a lot of time in front of the computer. "But you do, Mom," she said. I couldn't argue with her; I knew it was true. But I'm happy to say that the shame her comment elicited was just what I needed to turn over a new leaf. By the grace of God, I've been able to recognize that there are many things — not evils in and of themselves — that can become idols if we're not careful to seek God on a daily basis.

CHAPTER 4

I Love Your Life!

Did you know that the very moment the nomadic sperm cell plants its flag, so to speak, in the now-fertilized egg, there's an explosion and intertwining of DNA that will never be duplicated again? It has begun. A new life is forming at a miraculous rate. In the safety of the mother's womb, God's handiwork matures and develops. Each month shows new signs that all of nature's forces are working at a feverish pace to bring forth this unique life into the world.

First month — This new creation has a beating heart and a very simple spinal cord. Her eyes and ears are beginning to show. *God, I pray that when my daughter watches me, she learns not so much by my words but by my example, to live a life worth imitating.*

Second month — Internal organs are developing and

muscles are starting to move. Your son can express likes and dislikes by kicking and jerking. *God, help me to be sensitive to my son's wishes and not force my agenda onto him.*

Third month — Arms, hands, fingers, and toes are fully formed. Her little lips open and close. *Oh, God, when my daughter needs a hand to hold, please let me be there to comfort her. I commit to walking with her though life. Hand in hand.*

Fourth month — The ribs are clearly visible. Your son is approximately seven inches long. He can frown, squint, and grimace. *When my child has a sad face, make me caring and wise to bring Your light to his heart. And when he smiles, may I be there to laugh with him.*

Fifth month — Hair is beginning to appear on your daughter's head. Her ears are nearly complete, and she no longer lives in a silent, aquatic world. Outside noises and voices are reaching her ears. *You've counted every hair on her head, Lord. Help me to love her like You do.*

Sixth month — By now, your child is just about one pound. He has eyelashes and fingernails. He hears clearly and can move his body to the rhythm of your speech. *Oh, Lord, please give me the grace to use my tongue well. Keep me from words that shame and deflate my son's spirit. Help me to speak words of love, safety, and encouragement into the ears that You formed.*

Seventh month — Your daughter can sense or feel her mother's emotions at this point. Within a fraction of a second of a mother experiencing fear, the baby's heart starts pounding twice as fast. *God, in advance, I ask You to protect my child from any emotional trauma that the world may throw her way. May she grow in peace with a strong assurance of my love for her. And Yours.*

> Before I formed you in the womb, I knew you, and before you came to birth I consecrated you.
> JEREMIAH 1:5 (NJB)

Eighth month — The neural circuits in the brain are as advanced as a newborn's. Your baby is consciously aware. His brain is on the move. The sleeping and waking states are distinct. *Bless his mind, Lord. Help me to feed his impressionable brain with Your truths. I want him to think like a Christian.*

Ninth month — At the end of this final month of development, all of your baby's systems are simply striving to reach peak performance … she's getting geared up to thrive in the outside world. She has grown from the size of a pea to an average size of twenty inches and seven pounds. It's showtime! *This is it, God. We've been waiting and praying for nine months now. I know that I'm not totally ready, but I say yes to this child You've given us. I commit her life to You. You've done your part. Now help me to raise her. To love her. And to bring her close to You. Fill up in her what I lack. Amen.*

Life is so precious, and, in the grand scheme of things, so incredibly short. I'll never forget the first birthday I had without my mom. I was turning twelve. Those tumultuous teenage years would be here before I could blink. It was right around Christmastime when my mom passed away. Leukemia extinguished her flame. It was sudden. Tragic. Our family was utterly devastated. She was the light of my life.

My grandmother, God bless her, did everything she could to make my birthday special that dark January. There was extra "everything." She went overboard to pile on the cake, ice cream, and presents. Yet I clearly remember staring at those twelve candles and barely having the breath to blow them out. I had received one massive, heartbreaking shot to the solar plexus. I was numb ... gasping for air ... alone. All I wanted was my mom.

I was richly blessed to have had almost twelve years with my mom. No exaggerations here — she was very human, I know. But whatever shortcomings she had, she made up for by loving me well. I remember countless times when she'd seek me out, tenderly rub my shoulder, and say, "Hey, honey, do you wanna read a bit?" Even at ten and eleven years old, I relished the chance to be with her.

One day we were going through a book on gnomes. For some reason, these mythical short guys fascinated me, so my mom, in her motherly wisdom, bought a book that we could explore together. We read about gnome traditions, gnomes living in the forest, and gnomes fighting battles with tiny axes. To this day, I can't remember what intrigued me so much, but after our special reading session, I spontaneously exclaimed, "That is so cool, Mom!" She giggled and squeezed me while rocking me to and fro playfully.

"Oh, honey," she smiled. (Did I tell you that she had the greatest smile?) I saw her gazing at me, loving me with her beautiful, green eyes. Then she smattered me with a flurry of kisses all over my neck, forehead, and cheeks. I couldn't escape from her love.

"You know something?" she asked, brushing her hand through my hair.

"What?"

"I just love your life," she said so tenderly. "Don't ever forget that. ... I love your life."

Those simple words were engraved into my heart,

mind, and soul by a divine hand. Later, in times of my deepest grief and despair, I held onto them. For dear life. I knew she meant it, and her verbal blessing of my life allowed me to press on as I grew into adulthood and charted a new course of my own.

Do you want to raise a terrific Christian kid? Giving birth (moms, don't hate me for saying this, but here it comes) is really the easy part. Your son needs to know in the core of his heart that you are madly in love with his very life. You're his first glimpse of God. Bet your bottom dollar that the way *you* love him is the way he thinks *God* loves him, too. Your son knows that you see his good side and his bad side. He longs to know that despite all of it, you love the whole package.

Isn't that what we are basically saying every time we wish someone a happy birthday? I mean, think about it. We all take the same road to get onto this planet. We're card-carrying members of the aquatic womb club. And then, after nine tranquil months, we venture out into the world. On this earth, we all do some great things and some not-so-great things. On a birthday, there's a sort of unspoken acknowledgment that the birthday boy is incredibly imperfect, but for the day at least, it doesn't matter. An eternal truth lies hidden in our *Happy Birthday* chorus. We know that despite his shortcomings, this person was fearfully and wonderfully made. That God loves his life. And we're supposed to as well.

Let's roll up our sleeves...

TAKE STOCK. Think back to your childhood for a moment. Don't freak out on me here. I'm not at all suggesting you need to get on a couch, pay someone $85 an hour, and talk about how messed up you are because your dad didn't acknowledge your report card the right way. There are enough books out there encouraging you to be a victim, to blame all your personality quirks and habitual sins on your dysfunctional family life. Not here.

I do realize that some people truly were victims who had no positive parental interaction. But for the rest of you, just give me a few minutes and think back to a moment in your life when your mom and dad communicated to you, in some way, just how much they loved your life. It might have been on your birthday, on a vacation, or through a letter when you sat homesick in the college dormitory. Don't just think about it; get out a pen and write it down:

I recall feeling that my mom and dad really loved my life when: _____

_____

_____

_____

_____ .

Ponder the positive impact this one event had on you. How did it feed your self-confidence? Your ability to face an uncertain future? Get my point here? Now, do me a favor. If your mom or dad is still alive, throw this silly book on the floor and give 'em a call. Thank them for depositing this affirmation of your life into your impressionable memory. If they've passed away, offer your gratitude up in a personal prayer. And if you truly were never affirmed, decide now that your child will not experience the same negativity.

TAKE ACTION. It must be my Type A personality, because this is always my favorite section. This is where we really roll up the sleeves and get to work. Don't delay. Your child's heart is waiting for you.

❖ **Celebrate birthdays like never before!** Families have their various birthday traditions: a certain cake, streamers, maybe even a piñata. Let's bypass that stuff for a moment and get to the crux of the day — we're celebrating not just the day your son was born but his entire life!

- Have the entire family make signs that state things each person loves about the birthday boy. Then hang these in the place where everyone spends the most time. For example: *I love your smile, Johnny!* Or: *I love your caring heart!*

  Here are my two favorites: *Johnny, I am so glad you were born! I love your life!* That pretty much covers it, doesn't it?

Can a woman forget her infant, be without tenderness for the child of her womb? Even should she forget, I will never forget you.
ISAIAH 49:15-16

- Beyond cake and presents, give him some special time on his birthday. Contrary to what some books on childhood development say, there's really no substitute for quality time. The sky's the limit here. Pull out the old photo album and chuckle over your little man in his birthday suit. Go out for a long breakfast and talk about his interests. Sprinkle into the conversation just how much you love being his parent. And how much you love him just for being him. Let him know you're excited about his life. And that, despite his imperfections, you and God think he's downright terrific.

❖ **Give your son or daughter a feast day.** Each one of our eight children has a second day out of the year that is uniquely special. It's treated kind of like a birthday. He gets presents, cake and ice cream, and affirming signs galore. But this day is a little different. You see, when our children were born, we named them after saints — their own personal Christian heroes. The feast day is celebrated on a day assigned by the Church — usually, but not always, on the anniversary of the saint's death.

ROLL UP YOUR SLEEVES RESOURCES

- *The Power of a Praying Parent,* by Stormie Omartian
- *Words Kids Need to Hear,* by David Staal
- Any of the *Vision Books* series of saints' lives (Ignatius Press)

Take our son Gus, for example. This handsome eight-year-old has a million-dollar smile — especially now that his two front teeth have been handed over to the Tooth Fairy. His namesake walked this very earth approximately sixteen hundred years ago.

St. Augustine lived in Africa and had some rather
wild adolescent years. His mother stormed heaven
for her son's conversion. When Augustine finally
yielded his soul and mind to God's grace, the world
received a man of tremendous intellect who impacted
all of Christianity. His feast day is August 28, so
that has become a special day for Gus as well.

The way my wife and I figure it, the birthday rejoices
in the actual birth and life of our kids. The feast day
celebration rejoices in the Christian life to be lived
and the life that is yet to come when we meet our
Father in heaven. The feast day reminds each child
that he is part of a much larger family. The men
and women who have gone before us and lived
heroic lives of Christian virtue remind us that we,
too, are called to live for the Father.

For really, our time here on earth is similar to our
time in the womb — it's pretty darn short compared
with the eternal life that awaits all of us who have
given our hearts and lives to Christ.

TAKE TIME TO PRAY. "But you don't know what I've
been through!" some people have said to me. "My
parents never did any of that stuff. I was neglected,
abused, and brushed aside." I don't want to underestimate the emotional trauma one can acquire

from a hurtful experience. As a social worker, I dealt with some serious woundedness, and God knows I've spent a tremendous amount of time healing from my mom's sudden death.

On the flip side, I've also had some parents approach me with insurmountable mounds of guilt and self-condemnation heaped upon their souls. "I've been such a lousy parent. I've said hurtful things, been caught up in my own world for most of the time. My son's already a teenager, and I think it's too late. I blew it!"

Regardless of what happened when you were a kid or of your failings as a parent, don't lose sight of the fact that you and your child belong to Christ. He is the one who is faithful all the time.

Pray through any sufferings you endured. Talk to your Father in heaven, who, by the way, already knows about it all. Ask Him to help you forgive, heal, and move on. Despite what you have been through, the real tragedy would be staying stuck and not living or loving because of the pain you're holding on to.

Oh, Lord, I can't hold on to this pain any longer.
The resentment and bitterness is choking me.
My heart is so heavy. Take me into your arms, God.
Help me to know that you are a faithful Father.
Heal me. Restore me. Make me new.

And quit sentencing yourself as the world's most imperfect parent. Got a quick news flash for you — you *are* inadequate! You *will* hurt your child and let him down. There's no "Get out of sin and be a perfect parent" card. However, that doesn't mean that you should just plow through and hope for the best. No. God is calling you to something more.

Back to the title of this book. Terrific Christian parents typically raise terrific Christian kids. When you mess up, there's something basic you can do: Just admit it. *Joe, I can't believe I talked to you that way. I was angry with the fact that you didn't take out the garbage, but I really took it too far. I'm sorry.* That simple, ordinary confession not only throws balm on your son's hurt spirit, but it also teaches him that even good-hearted Christians mess up. Ask for forgiveness and move on! Make sense?

Oh, and one last thought, dear reader. We've talked at length in this chapter about your children. I would be remiss not to turn the table on you for just a moment. We busy adults sometimes forget God's simple truths. Our Father in heaven, the Creator of all things good and beautiful, has counted every hair on your head, too. Yup, He was there the precise moment you were conceived. He struck up the band as all of heaven rejoiced.

Our Eternal Father has been with you in good times and in bad. Your first steps. The first time you prayed the *Our Father* from memory. Your wedding day. Remember that flat tire in the rain? How about the time you sat alone in your room, lost in tears because your first crush went with someone else to the dance? And when your company downsized, and you fell behind on the bills? Yup, He was there as you stared despairingly at the checkbook balance. He's always been there, loving you with a perfect love.

Don't worry — His affection for you hasn't dropped off over the years like your metabolism. He doesn't care about receding hairlines, varicose veins, 401ks, golf handicaps, and your Buick. You'll always be the apple of His eye. He created your soul. You're His kid. And I just gotta tell you something:

He loves your life!

Reflections from Dad...

"Hey, Daddy," my son said excitedly as he held his Star Wars Yoda figurine in his hand. I was tucking him in after a long, stimulating day.

"What, bud?" I asked, secretly wondering if his adrenal glands would finally shut down so he could fall asleep.

"This was the best birthday ever!" He beamed.

I reflected on the day's events for a moment while he and Yoda battled Darth Vader with light sabers.

Our birthday boy rose in the morning to see a myriad of handmade signs plastered throughout the kitchen. All of his siblings had contributed to the artistic display. "Hooray, it's Peter's birthday!" read one of them. Another had Peter's name decorated in a variety of colors while stick figures with ropes and guns traversed all over it. He thought that was particularly cool. Since I was the inspired artist, I agreed wholeheartedly.

His mother and I then took him out for breakfast.

Just the three of us. A special meal for an out-of-the-ordinary day. "Go ahead, sweetheart," his mother said. "Order whatever you want — this is your day."

Peter flashed a wide grin. "Even the pancakes with M&Ms?" he inquired with a hopeful tone. "That sounds like a Jedi breakfast to me," I chimed in. "Go for it, young Skywalker." Peter feasted, and my wife and I thanked God for this five-year-old boy who was so full of life. He left the birthday breakfast with a green helium balloon and a spirit that soared.

"Tacos!" Peter raucously announced to the family when asked what he wanted for his birthday dinner. And that's what we ate that night. It was his call. At grace, we took a few extra moments to thank God for so generously giving us Peter. We thanked Him for Peter's Type A personality, his love of sports, and various other qualities that we all loved about the birthday boy. The man of the hour dined on his favorite meal, and we all enjoyed it with him.

His presents were wrapped and placed in secret hiding spots throughout the living room. We cheered as he explored the room in search of his gifts. To this day, I think my kids have more fun finding their gifts than actually receiving them.

Of course, Mom made a special Star Wars cake, adorned with the Yoda figurine, and we sang Happy Birthday loud and clear.

Construction paper, crayons, breakfast, some basic presents, and a homemade cake — certainly nothing extraordinary or expensive. But love and celebration for his life made the day magical. "Yeah, Pete. It was perfect," I said brushing his hair with my hand. "God sure did a great job when He made you."

I thought of my Mom, then passed the words on to him that she had so generously given to me. I looked directly into my son's eyes. "Hey, birthday boy," I whispered. "You know what? I love your life."

His eyes sparkled and his face shone. "Thanks, Daddy," he said. "I love your life, too."

Reflections from Mom...

I love to "love on" my kids. I can't help myself. From the first moment that the first baby was laid on my chest, before the cord was even cut, I just had to envelop that little being in my arms and cover his downy little head with kisses. I had to stop wearing lipstick because it would always end up on the kids instead of me.

I cannot hold my children without kissing them, or rubbing their backs, or stroking their little hands in mine. I think God, in His wisdom, created me this way to make up for the fact that verbal affirmation does not come naturally to me. But our third child, Johnny, taught me that I need to be verbal as well.

Johnny was the child who did not want to be smothered. When he was a baby, he needed the physical contact, but on his terms, which meant him lying right on my chest, not enveloped in my arms. That way he was in control and had freedom to move.

When he started talking, I noticed that he would

ask for verbal affirmation or state it himself, saying things like, "Mommy loves Johnny," or "Do you love me?" Even now, at eleven years old, he approaches me two or three times a day, gives me a hug, and says, "I love you, Mom."

It finally dawned on me that he was trying to tell me what he needed from me, how he needed me to love him. So even though it's not second nature to me, I've learned to tell all my children verbally that I love them and think they're great, and that I love being their mom.

If there's one thing I've realized having eight children, it's how different they are from each other. So I figure if I speak love in as many languages as I can, they will each get the message.

CHAPTER 5

Bite Your Tongue!

S it back with me for a minute while I turn on the black-and-white television set. Don't worry. You can still enjoy your Salisbury steak TV dinner as we tune in. Let me set the scene for you, circa 1953. Mom is where most moms were in the '50s — the kitchen. Her hair is immaculate, almost sculpted. She has to be careful near the stove's pilot light, because one spark could cause her thickly hair-sprayed cranium to resemble a flaming marshmallow gone bad at the campfire. Her white apron squeezes her tiny waist like a tourniquet.

Junior enters stage right. The door swings noisily as he strolls in, baseball glove in hand, chomping a wad of bubble gum at a happy-go-lucky pace. Except Mama's little boy isn't too happy this sunny Saturday afternoon in small-town Americana.

Our 1950's mom diligently tends to the pork chops in the frying pan. Junior sits down and throws his baseball cap on the red-and-white checkered tablecloth. Mom hands him a glass of milk and two chocolate-chip cookies.

OK, you with me so far? The stage is set. Now here comes the dialogue:

"How was your ballgame, dear?" She refills his glass of milk.

"Shucks, Mom, it was a real drag. That stupid Jimmy Smith belted a winning home run off of me. I can't pitch worth a lick!"

"I'm sorry, hon, there's always the next ballgame." Mom flips the sizzling chops and begins to spoon out homemade applesauce into patterned bowls.

"Forget about it, Mom! I'm sick of baseball, and I'm even more sick of Jimmy! Just wait, 'cause next time I'm going to plant a baseball right in his big fat ear!"

"Junior!" Mom leaves the chops and approaches her son with both hands resting on her eighteen-inch waist. "Now, I can understand you're upset about losing, but ..."

Junior cuts her off, clearly unable to stop reliving his poor pitching performance. "It's not just losing, Mom. It's ... it's losing to that no-good, big-eared, metal-mouth, stupid, Jimm ..."

At this point in the story, the chops are left to burn on the pan. Our 1950's mom is about to fry something else. She grabs the fatty part of her son's ear and walks him to the sink. She clearly won't stand for this sassy talk. Not in her kitchen. No, sir.

Realizing that her son is lost in anger, frustration, and a huge absence of basic manners, she has to bring out the big guns.

"Junior, bite your tongue!" she says. "Right now! I've heard enough coming out of that mouth. One more negative, mean word and I'll wash your mouth out with soap! Am I clear? Do yourself a big favor and bite your tongue! Just wait 'til your father comes home!"

We all chuckle at this scene from an American childhood. We've come a long way in our society. Haven't we? TV sets are now high-def with amazing color clarity. Instead of the belt or Junior chewing on some Ivory soap, we now have timeout chairs and counselors recommending that Junior sets his own punishment. And heck, have you looked in the nearest frozen-food aisle lately? TV dinners are now like 5-star meals (but still nothing like mom's pork chops).

Although times have changed, and, in theory, life is supposed to have gotten better, one thing has remained pretty constant — misuse of the tongue can get all of us in a heap of trouble. I know your kids will agree with me on this one.

If there's a "physician, heal thyself" chapter in this book, for me, it's this one. Unlike my wife, I'm a natural-born talker. My extroverted personality compels me to dole out comments and thoughts rapidly and, well, often without much thought. From time to time, I allow too much to spill off my tongue, and so, unlike my dear wife, I find myself regretting words that fly out of my mouth.

I distinctly remember the day I realized my tongue was as undisciplined as a cackling hyena. I was a sophomore in college and found myself discussing my "tongue ailment" with a wise Franciscan priest. His hair was white as snow and contrasted perfectly with his brown robe. He held the end of his rope cord, which rested loosely around his jolly belly, in his weathered hand.

"James," he said thoughtfully. "Have you read it?"

"James… as in the Bible?" I responded, feeling rather foolish. At the age of nineteen, I was anything but a Bible-carrying Christian. I wasn't even sure where to find James. "It's in the New Testament, right?" I continued hesitantly, hoping this holy man wouldn't see my ignorance.

"Don't worry," he said, seeming to sense my uneasiness. "We'll find it together."

As this smiling Franciscan paged through a well-used Bible, I wondered just how many other students he had shepherded so gently.

"Here, it is. Good ol' James," he said with the same tone you'd hear a veteran using when reminiscing about a fallen comrade. "Ah, how I've tried and tried to be faithful to the words in these four chapters. That's all there are, you know — just four. Compared with all that's in this good book," — he held up the Bible — "James is like a teardrop in God's vast ocean. And yet," he looked at me intently, "if you dare to read James and be faithful to it, you'll be counted among God's greatest saints."

"You ready?" he asked as if we were about to plunge out of a plane at fifteen thousand feet for a tandem parachute ride. He read prayerfully:

> For every kind of beast and bird, of reptile and sea creature, can be tamed and has been tamed by the human species, but no human being can tame the tongue. It's a restless evil, full of deadly poison. With it we bless the Lord and Father, and with it we curse men, who are made in the likeness of God. From the same mouth come blessing and cursing. This need not be so, my brothers.
>
> JAMES 3:7-10

"Well, what do you think of your new friend James?" he asked with a witty smile.

"Umm, pretty clear," I said with a dry throat, seriously wondering if James had had me in mind when he and God wrote those words.

"Yeah," he sighed, seeming to understand the spiritual mountain I was about to tackle. "And that's just three sentences. Take this Bible. Read James. Pray over it, and let every word sink into your heart and mind. Be obedient to it."

"OK, thanks," I said, secretly wondering if I had the wherewithal to do what he asked.

"One more thing," he said as he playfully slapped my shoulder. "If you try with all your heart to use your tongue wisely, you'll still mess up and fall. Trust me, I'm an expert on this," he said with a chuckle. "Promise me you won't fret over it. Ask our merciful Father for forgiveness and help. And whatever you do, keep climbing!"

Let's roll up our sleeves...

TAKE STOCK. All right, all right, enough about me and my imperfections. Let's talk about something that makes me a bit more comfortable — let's talk about you! I know, I know, you're probably wondering when we're gonna hit on your kids and their misuse of the tongue. We'll get there. In case you haven't already noticed, the guy penning these words believes that if you want to change your kids, you need to start with the parental hands holding this book.

I can think of no other area where children will so

quickly imitate their parents than in the matter of speech. Let's get to the bottom line: If they hear you do it — swear, gossip, lie, berate, shame, humiliate, murmur, criticize, disgrace, and condemn — your kids will follow suit. The oddsmakers in Vegas would say it's a sure bet.

> *I fear that I will be held accountable*
> *for the way I used my tongue.*
>
> ST. MARIA FAUSTINA

Show me a boy who curses, and I'll bet he heard those words from dear old Dad when the team lost the football game in the final two minutes. Show me a girl who gossips about her friends, and I'll bet my bottom dollar she's witnessed Mom and Aunt Susie sharing a cup of coffee while gossiping about the neighbor, the annoying cousin, and the Joneses' marital problems.

Don't forget — if your kids hear you use words that praise, invoke honor, encourage, absolve, hearten, compliment, admire, express approval, and bless, well, you know what the Vegas oddsmakers say will happen. The apple doesn't ever really fall too far from the tree, does it?

We've all known at least one neighbor girl who says "please" and "no thank you" without being prompted.

We smile when we see a child who has been instructed to use her tongue properly, with class. It's refreshing, isn't it? Show me a boy who offers encouraging words to his brother when he strikes out, and you're not just pointing out admirable behavior between siblings. No, you're actually showing me a home that places a high priority on using the tongue to encourage, support, and build up — specifically in times when we walk back to the dugout of life, dragging our bat, feeling defeated and discouraged.

ROLL UP YOUR SLEEVES RESOURCES

- *Me and My Big Mouth,* by Joyce Meyer
- *Does Your Tongue Need Healing?* by Derek Prince
- *There's Power in Your Tongue,* by Maria Vadia

This is not an easy topic to breeze through. If God faxed you a Christian Parent Job Description, well, based on "good ol' James," it's safe to say that one of your Major Responsibilities would look something like this:

❖ Train your children to use their tongues in ways that glorify God. The first and foremost method in achieving this worthy end, you ask? Simple — teach by example.

There are no topic-related questions here for you

today. No allotted space for you to write out a reflection. By now, if you haven't taken an honest, hard look at the use of your tongue and your kids' tongues, I don't know what else to say. ("Hmmm," my wife chimes in from the peanut gallery, "that's a first!")

TAKE ACTION. All too often, we recognize our sin and then we sit around and mope about it. We hold on to the realization of our sinfulness as if it's something to be treasured. Self-pity is not a virtue. Remember what the wise Franciscan Friar said to me: "Promise me you won't fret over it. Ask our merciful Father for forgiveness and help. And whatever you do, keep climbing!"

The following three action points are aimed at helping you grow in awareness and maturity in your speech. Consider them climbing tools.

❖ **Make James your best friend.** C'mon, there are only four small chapters to cover. Plant yourself down and admit that the author of this book isn't the only one who could benefit from being obedient to the spiritual discipline of taming the tongue. Read these four chapters with your children. Read them with laser-like focus, and read them over and over again. Then pray. And I mean hard. Hold your son's hand as you pray that all the members of your family grow in self-control of this "little thing" in their mouths that has the power to bless and curse.

❖ **Take the "4:29 Challenge."** Get yourself on the computer and print out the following Scripture verse in big, bold letters:

> *Let no evil talk come out of your mouths, but only what is useful for building up, as there is need, so that your words may give grace to those who hear.*
>
> EPHESIANS 4:29

Great — now put this in a very prominent place. Sit down with the entire family and commit this awesome sentence to memory. Now, commit to taking the "4:29 Challenge." The rules are simple. When someone catches you slipping with your tongue, they need to gently point it out by saying, "Ah, 4:29."

By the way, moms and dads, be prepared to get called out by your kids.

❖ **The "Three Rs."** This is one of my favorite spiritual-action items. The "Three Rs" is a simple spiritual reminder of what you need to do when you've messed up with your tongue.

Allow me to illustrate:

I'm driving my family home from church and without even realizing it, I blurt out a sarcastic comment about the soloist in the choir loft. "4:29!" somebody shouts from the rear of the car. I feel like I was just pelted by a spiritual dodge ball. "Unbelievable," I mutter in total annoyance with myself. "Five minutes out of church and my tongue is already a loose cannon." Let me share with you a three-step approach that will effectively help you respond to your tongue mishaps:

The "Three Rs"

R#1: Repent. Lord, I'm so sorry. I can't believe I just made a useless comment about that person. And I did it in front of my kids. I don't want to be that kind of example, Lord. It's so arrogant to speak that way. I fully repent of it, Lord.

R#2: Revoke. Lord, I revoke what I said. I un-say it. I spiritually take those worthless words back. I don't want them falling on anyone.

R#3: Replace. Lord, I replace those words with a blessing. I thank you for this woman. You love her just as much as you love me and my kids. Help me to remember that. I bless her, Lord. I bless her life and her heart that sings to you. Please bless her, God.

TAKE TIME TO PRAY. Just think for a moment on all that Jesus could have said during his three hours on the cross. He was, in fact, on an elevated pulpit. The entire world was looking up at Him. You don't need to be a Scripture scholar to note that He didn't go on a "Shame on you!" rant to all of those folks who twisted and distorted His message. Further, not once did He bitterly cry out, "I know who you are ... you did this to Me! You'll be sorry. This cuts you off from Me and My Father. You had your chance. You're done."

Books have been written by medical doctors, historians, and theologians who have studied, in-depth, the tortuous science of crucifixion. The Romans were no grass-roots hate group. They knew exactly how to crucify someone in a way that would create the most pain and suffering. The guillotine, firing squad, and the like are "walks in the park" compared with the way of the cross.

Our Lord willingly placed himself in the hands of skilled torturers. Nails were strategically placed to hit the large nerve that extended to the back of the head. Any movement of the arm or hand ignited a fiery explosion along the nerve pathway. Shoulders were dislocated. And breathing ... well, that's something we take for granted because it happens without notice. Not so on the cross. Since his diaphragm was constricted because of his position, Jesus needed to push up with his feet to breathe. The weight of his thirty-three-year-old frame had to push against the nail holding him to the wood. Get the picture?

If it took that much work to breathe, imagine the effort involved in speaking even a few words. So we'd best take notice of the words our omniscient God chose to speak during His last three hours on earth. For those of you who don't speak Aramaic or don't have a theology degree, allow me to give you the cliff-note version of what He did and didn't do with His tongue:

Jesus didn't scold, curse, shame, lecture, or wish anyone ill will.

Jesus did pray with His heart to the Father. He promised a convicted criminal that he would have eternal life in Paradise. He expressed concern and love for His mother. He forgave us and asked His Father to do the same.

Even as my fingertips hit the keyboard, I wonder if I've said too much. This topic needs to be "prayed about" more than it needs to be "talked about." So let's do that:

Oh, God, please give me a new tongue. You see how often I mess up. I know that my kids are watching my example. Help me to give them a good one. When I fall short, please give me the humility to admit it and to seek You. I need your help, Lord. Help me to bless and not to curse. And help me to form and instruct them to use their tongues in ways that glorify You. Amen.

The next time you're sitting down to a scrumptious TV dinner or watching *Leave it to Beaver* reruns, think good and hard when the 1950's mom takes hold of Junior's ear and speaks with appropriate parental concern: "Bite your tongue!" We viewers — young and old alike — best heed her motherly advice. For us Christians, it's not "just wait 'til your father comes home" but rather "just wait 'til you go home to the Father." It's in the heavenly kitchen of our Father's house where you and I and our children will each have a good long talk about the ways we used our tongues here on earth.

Reflections from Dad

It was Monday morning, and my week was already off to a bad start. My voice mail had two messages from key clients who had to cancel. I was late for a conference call and couldn't eat breakfast because my shirt required ironing. I violently poured some coffee into a travel mug and frantically rummaged for something to eat. In my hurry, I accidentally stepped on the dog's paw. He yelped. I turned and hastily knocked over my mug. A slew of negative words poured out of my mouth.

As hot coffee cascaded waterfall-like onto the floor, my son's soft voice drew me in. It was Johnny. He sat at the kitchen table, oblivious to my frenzied state. In his nine-year-old hand he embraced a pastel-colored index card. He was reading from it.

I recognized it instantly. These affirming words came from a Joel Osteen book. My wife and I thought it would be formative for the kids to write them out and repeat them. Every morning. And that's exactly what

Johnny was doing, while the dog licked his paw, and I paused to listen.

"I am valuable and I am loved. God's blessings are chasing me down and overtaking me. Everything I touch prospers and succeeds. I am excited about my future."

He then placed the card on the table and dutifully proceeded to start his homework.

There's something so life-changing about positive words. Especially when they are spoken out loud. His voice breathed hope and perspective into my morning rush. The tongue can be used to curse the dog and the spilled coffee, to be sure, but it can also be employed to right the course of my ship. Positive, grateful, and expectant words are like a favorable wind to the downtrodden sailor.

"Hey, bud," I spoke, interrupting his studies. "Can I borrow your card? I think your old man needs to speak those words. Maybe a few times," I said, feeling a little more lighthearted as I stroked the dog.

"Yeah, Dad, sure," he said with a smile.

Reflections from Mom

It was the day of a big party — a thirtieth wedding anniversary bash for my parents. After trying on several dresses, both my own and my sister's, I finally settled on the only one in which I didn't feel totally unattractive.

I emerged from my room — somewhat self-consciously, as I had a houseful of people — and made my way toward the living room, where my two-and-a-half-year-old son, Joseph, was engrossed in play. As I clicked down the hallway in my high heels, Joe suddenly looked up from his trucks and audibly gasped, ran to me, and exclaimed, "Oh, Mommy, you look so pretty!" As tears sprang to my eyes, all I could do was hug the little cherub.

After the chaos of the day was over, that moment was still embedded in my mind. In fact now, twelve years later, I can still vividly recall it. What joy it had given me simply to hear my son exclaim over me with such excitement and sincerity. Words can be so powerful. In his childlike purity, my son had naturally chosen to use his words to bless his mommy. I pray that my own example will continue to nurture this natural tendency in all of my children.

CHAPTER 6

Purity Ring

Imagine a man who has great wealth, power, and influence. One who is esteemed by most of the world, his popularity unparalleled. Or picture the tan, blond-haired, blue-eyed captain of the varsity football team. All the girls want to be his date at the prom. He's in the "cool" crowd. Now magnify these images by a million.

This man has the Midas touch. He's a stud. Prosperity is his best friend. He's never had to comb through the self-help section in Barnes & Noble hoping to find the one book that will finally help him reach his goals. He's marinated in success. Dignitaries and common folk alike respect and envy his life. He just has that "it" we talk about whenever a remarkable person comes up in conversation.

You with me? Good. Now imagine this exemplary model of human achievement choosing to throw "it" all away for sexual impurity's empty promises. No, I'm not talking about the latest political scandal on CNN. This man is light years ahead of an ordinary state governor. "Must be some star athlete or Hollywood heartthrob," you ponder. Guess again. This is no grocery-store tabloid.

I'm talking about David. You know, one of the greatest figures found in the Old Testament. Remember the underdog youngster who whipped the ominous giant with a killer slingshot? Yeah, that David. God always had a unique plan for this sheep herder. David started out standing up to the local bully and ended up a king. A true rags-to-riches story. And David knew it, too.

God's favor just seemed to follow David through life. He really did have it all. But in spite of all the wealth, fame, and heavenly assistance, our friend royally blew it. He was trained under the law of Moses. Unlike today, the Ten Commandments were truly written in stone. No picking and choosing which of the ten David liked and didn't like. God's law was clear. Especially when it came to the area of sexual purity. And David knew that, too.

And yet, for some strange reason, he chose to covet what did not belong to him. Check it out for yourself in 2 Samuel 11-12. His eyes wandered. He wanted something that was not rightfully his. Lies followed. Manipulations. One big step away from God, and David tumbled miserably down a slippery slope of sin. His lack of self-control was nothing less than a slap in the face to the God who had been so faithful and generous to Him. God even said so through his spokesman, Nathan. Take a listen:

> I anointed you king of Israel. I rescued you from the hand of Saul. I gave you your lord's house and your lord's wives for your own. I gave you the house of Israel and of Judah. And if this were not enough, I could count up for you still more. Why have you spurned the LORD and done evil in his sight?
>
> 2 SAMUEL 12:7-9

"Unbelievable!" you say in amazement, perplexed that a man of such stature and blessing would be so foolish. "How could someone be so short-sighted? So selfish? So downright stupid?" I join you in the chorus. And then, you and I pause. In a blink, we remember asking these very same questions while we stared in the mirror.

I would be a fool to pen a book on Christian parenting without touching upon sexual purity. Secular authors have filled countless books with theories, commentaries, and educated opinions on the subject. Not here. Not today. You and I are stuck to the confines of one chapter. So let's swallow our awkwardness and get talking.

I was eleven when I first realized that girls didn't look all that bad. It was right around the onset of MTV. Hormones and the videos on that channel — mmm, not a good mix, if you know what I mean. It was around that same time that I discovered a hidden cupboard in my house. It's not what you think. When I happened upon that secret hideaway, I found my parents' Christmas stash. Yup, this is where they stored the still-unwrapped presents.

"I struck gold!" I giggled with yuletide glee, knowing that I would get a sneak peak at what was to come. It was only two days before Christmas, yet I was able to enjoy the gifts that were set aside for me — now! In case you're curious, my favorite item was a Cleveland Browns football jersey. The very one I had been longing to get for as long as I could remember. Excited, I put it on. When nobody was looking. In secret. I felt older. Cool. Like a champ. It was awesome. "This will be the best Christmas ever!" I shouted to my empty house, quickly putting the gift back before anyone caught me.

It was early morning when I skipped into the kitchen and popped open the perforated December 25 box on the Advent calendar. "Christmas is here!" I joyfully called out to my sleeping family. They all came down, still in their pajamas, not wanting to delay the event we had all been anticipating. At last, the moment had arrived.

"Merry Christmas, guys," my mom said cheerfully, lost in her puffy bathrobe and stirring a cup of tea. "Let's get going."

My older brother went first. Then it was my turn.

"Showtime," I said with an all- knowing smile.

"Here, sweetheart, open this one first," my mom said. "We know you're going to like it!" She handed me the box. It was perfectly wrapped. The dark red paper complemented the ivy-green bow. I shook the package, wondering aloud about its contents. I was playing the part. My parents looked excited to see me open my special gift.

And then I opened it. Of course it was the Browns jersey. The very one I had tried on and enjoyed over and over again these last couple of days. "What's wrong with you, man?" my brother asked inquisitively. "You've been wanting that jersey for years. Don't look so unhappy." I mustered up a smile as best I could. It was forced. Unnatural. The jersey felt used. My spirit was flat.

At that very moment my conscience was playing the role of the three Wise Men. It had presented my heart, mind, and soul with three gifts that special Christmas: regret, guilt, and remorse.

Much older now, I can look back at that important Christmas morning and understand what had happened. You see, I had cheated that day. My secret searching out of gifts that weren't yet mine to use and enjoy was premature. Timing is everything. The moment was not right to enjoy the gift. Yet I did. On my terms. Because it felt right at the time. And I wanted to. Not only had I been deceitful to my parents, but I also had crossed a line. My young conscience had blown the whistle. And, like David, I knew it, too.

You gettin' my drift here? Of course, the Creator, in His infinite generosity, gave us a far greater gift than a silly old football jersey. You and I know that. And as your kids walk the rocky path called puberty, they'll realize that, too. There's just something so sacred about how we were created. Our gender and sexual expression are God's masterpieces. Just as Christmas gifts are meant to be opened on a specific day, so God has specific plans and appropriate times for the gift He has given us to be enjoyed.

In pursuit of a master's degree in social work, I logged in far too many hours hearing trained professionals and out-of-touch professors offer their infallible opinions on the "do's and don'ts" of this topic. But I prefer to go to the Source. To the One who is pure love and who created us in His very image.

The collegiate orators say sex outside of marriage is fine. The Creator of your soul, however, seems to have a different take:

> *B*e sure of this, that no immoral or impure, or greedy person, that is, an idolater, has any inheritance in the kingdom of God. Let no one deceive you with empty arguments . . .
>
> EPHESIANS 5:5-6

The intellectuals hate that last sentence. Popular

opinion boldly endorses practiced homosexuality, pornography, premarital sex, and on and on. "C'mon, get with the times," the world whispers in your child's ear. "We aren't in the Middle Ages anymore. There are no absolutes." Funny, the One who has breathed life into your very soul begs to differ:

> Do not be deceived; neither fornicators, nor idolaters, nor adulterers, nor practicing homosexuals, nor thieves, nor the greedy, nor drunkards, nor slanderers, nor robbers will inherit the kingdom of God.
>
> 1 CORINTHIANS 6:9-10

Desperate, feeling pushed in a corner, the voice of the masses snaps back, "Don't tell me what to do with my body. It's up to me. My choice! I decide what's best." The voice lashes out in temper-tantrum fashion. Our Father, ever patient, gently lifts the chin of this rebellious child and speaks through His Apostle Paul:

> Avoid immorality. Every other sin that a person commits is outside the body, but the immoral person sins against his own body. Do you not know that your body is a temple of the Holy Spirit within you, whom you have from God, and that you are not your own? For you have been purchased at a price. Therefore glorify God in your body.
>
> 1 CORINTHIANS 6:18-20

Your children are one mouse click away from so many sexual images it would frighten Frankenstein. It's scary. Don't be deceived by the experts and the seductive voice of popular opinion. Not if you want to raise terrific Christian kids. Turn to the Bible. It's God's Word. And for heaven's sake, diligently place a protective ring of purity around your children's bodies and souls.

Let's roll up our sleeves...

TAKE STOCK. Given the significance of this topic and the overwhelming emphasis society places on it, I suggest that "taking stock" needs to happen on an ongoing basis. Let's go through a quick checklist. A conscious and honest taking of inventory, if you will:

When was the last time you checked to make sure your child was "clean and free" on the Internet? Date: _____

How about his cell phone? Date: _____

And the TV? Date: _____

When did you last sit down to have a loving conversation about Christian purity with your daughter? Date: _____

How often do you pray for your child's purity? Check one:

☐ Daily ☐ Weekly ☐ Monthly
☐ Gosh, never really thought about it.

Would you want your son or daughter to imitate the way you currently live out Christian purity?
☐ Yes or ☐ No

A good, hard, honest look at this area is key, but even more important is that you roll up your sleeves and deal with this with the same enthusiasm and determination you would use in planning a dream vacation.

TAKE ACTION.

❖ **Give your child a Purity Ring.** At an appropriate age — typically, the onset of puberty is a good time — have a special date with your child. Go out for dinner. To a nice place. When the waitress finally clears the empty sundae dish and your coffee cup, it's time to start talking. Your child needs to know that he's got "all access" to you regarding this topic. "Just pick up the Bat Phone," you say. You're never too busy to handle an awkward question or concern. It's what you do. There's no way your child is going to walk through puberty feeling alone. You're his mom. His dad. And this is important.

Head out to the mall or local Christian bookstore. You've called ahead to be sure "the item" is in stock. Lead your son and daughter to the Purity Ring section. Tell them to have at it. She likes the one with the Celtic cross and rose. "This is like a princess ring, Mom," she says with a grin. You smile. Perfect. He thinks the one with the cross and crown of thorns looks manly. "It's kinda like a ring that a knight would wear in *The Lord of the Rings* or something," he says with the face of a prince about to receive an award for his victorious battle against the dragon. You smile again. Perfect.

❖ **Be Papa Antivirus and Mama SpyWare.** Listen, you and I don't need a scientific study to show that kids today are completely overloaded with sexual images portraying unhealthy relationships and un-biblical beliefs. Now either you go entirely Amish on this one and forgo use of electricity, or you step up to the plate and make sure filth and smut aren't being down-loaded before your kid's eyes — the window to the soul. A few ideas:

1. Cell phones can be set to not accept text pictures.

2. Computers have parental controls and screening software. *Safeeyes.com is terrific.

ROLL UP YOUR SLEEVES RESOURCES

- *Every Young Man's Battle*, by Stephen Arterburn & Fred Stoecker

- *Every Young Woman's Battle*, by Stephen Arterburn & Shannon Ethridge

- *And the Bride Wore White*, by Dannah Gresh

3. Cable channels can be blocked.

❖ **Buy yourself a Purity Ring.** Before you leave that store, be sure to grab a purity ring for yourself, too. "We're in this together," you say as you place the ring on a simple chain to wear around your neck. There's no way your child will walk through the turbulent teen years alone. Not in your house. There's too much at stake. And there's no way you can ask them to live in purity if you're not. *Mmmphh*, forgive me as I clear my throat. Remember that whole "lead by example thing?" Yeah, that's REALLY BIG here.

The ring's purpose is to provide a visible reminder that your child's sexuality is a gift from God. We're to guard this gift. Protect it. And encourage them to enjoy it in God's good time. On the "big day," the ring is removed and replaced with a wedding band. You vividly remember the day she first put on her purity ring. She was so young. Now she's at the altar. Dressed in white. Your son looked so excited to don his manly jewelry. Now your future daughter-in-law slides a new ring on your little boy's finger. You smile yet again. Perfect.

ROLL UP YOUR SLEEVES RESOURCES

- *Did Adam & Eve Have Belly Buttons?* by Matt Pinto

- *Strong Fathers, Strong Daughters,* by Meg Meeker

- *Covenant of Love,* by Fr. Richard Hogan & John Levoir

So your purity ring serves as a reminder that one day, your child will most likely leave you and give himself to another in marriage. Your ring reminds you to pray. For your daughter's purity, to be sure, but also for her future spouse. Her prince is out there. Somewhere. He's on the baseball field or chasing the ice-cream truck. He's taking his driver's license test or surfing the Internet. Pray for his purity, too. Pray good and hard. I know you don't know his name. But God does.

It's funny; we parents spend a lot of time praying for things like:

- Johnny getting A's on his exams — *yet fifth grade only lasts ten months*

- Maggie making some friends at summer camp — *which lasts all but six days*

- Joe getting picked for All-Stars — *a two-day tournament*

And yet we never quite think about devoting a few minutes to pray for our son's future spouse — *an event designed to last a lifetime.*

TAKE TIME TO PRAY. Back to our friend David for a moment. Remember him? The psalmist turned voyeur. The blessed king turned conniver. Contrary to popular opinion, even back in the day, our Father wasn't a thunderbolt-throwing, white-bearded, cantankerous judge. Mercy is one of God's greatest attributes. Let me define it for you. It's really quite simple. Mercy is when God loves you, forgives you, and heals you — when you don't deserve it. There's nothing your finite little person can do to earn God's mercy. It's freely given.

David lost a battle waged between his flesh and God's

law, but he didn't lose the war. He repented and was forgiven. Many of us have been injured and have hurt others in our Christian call of duty. Sexual battle scars cover our troubled hearts. We've been beaten down by an endless barrage of enemy fire. Memories of regretful relationships and self-centered behaviors haunt us in traumatizing flashbacks. Nobody can truly cast the first stone at poor old David, 'cause, well, you know.

God knows, too. But remember what our main man David wrote in Psalm 136: *His mercy endures forever.* He sent His Son to pay for all your sins. And mine. Your kids' sins, too. Don't forget the key point Paul was trying to bring home: *You are not your own; you were bought with a price.* Jesus Christ willingly laid down His life so that we would be forgiven and received in heaven. Purity was spit upon, whipped, and brutally nailed to gnarled wood for our impurities. David understood God's mercy. Yet how easily we forget.

Oh, God, I know this is an area of huge importance in my Christian life. Forgive me for the times I've turned my back on You and walked in outright selfishness. I'm sorry, Lord, for those I have hurt because I opened Your gift prematurely and used it my way. Heal them, Lord. Heal me. Make all things new. Help me to walk in purity. I want to lead and protect my kids from anyone and anything that seeks to stain and rob their purity. Give me wisdom, Lord. Help me to talk to my kids. To safeguard them until the day they approach You in matrimony. I pray for my son's future spouse. You know who she is, Lord. Bless and protect her. Keep my future son-in-law safe. Prepare him for my daughter. Thank you for paying the price for me. And for my kids. Thank You for Your mercy. Amen.

All this chatter about gifts has gotten me in the Christmas spirit. It may be a humid August afternoon, but I just can't help myself. "Here!" I say with yuletide glee as I place a small, wrapped box in your hands. You chuckle because it's wrapped with the Sunday comics. I smile because I know what's inside. "Open it," I say.

"What's it for?" you rightfully ask. "It's not my birthday, you know."

"Like I even know when your birthday is," I retort impatiently.

"And Christmas is months away," you add, slapping

the pot-bellied mosquito on your tan arm.

"I know, I know, but the timing is perfect. Our chapter is coming to a close! Just open it already."

With a determined face you set out to remove the generously applied tape and paper. The small box cover lifts easily. A thin, cotton-like square is then pulled out of the box. Your eyes stare intently at the gift. "What ..." you start, but I cut you off.

"Just keep looking at the gift. Isn't it awesome? There's not another out there in all of creation. Handcrafted, I'm telling you. Delicate yet remarkably resilient. One of the Artist's finest masterpieces, if you ask me. I know He'd agree. Just utterly amazing," I say as you gaze in the little round mirror.

"Fearfully and wonderfully made," I pronounce with awe and reverence. He collaborated with your biological mom and dad to create the amazing gift we call you. Honor the Great Gift Giver. Use your gifts well. Form your kids according to His plan for Christian purity. Talk with them. Walk with them. Pray with them and for them. Take it from the guy who wore that old Cleveland Browns jersey twenty-nine years ago. And from David, one of God's wisest, who lived like royalty back in the day. Place a ring of purity around you and your family. Trust me on this. Your kids will thank you.

Reflections from Dad...

I honestly can't remember which father-daughter dance it was. They all blend together into one, big, sweet, honkin' memory. For years, my daughter Maggie and I would dress up on some cold, gray Saturday around Valentine's Day and attend our special dance.

Now that I think of it, she must have been around six. I don't know, maybe it was seven. Mom had prepared her hair just right. Her brown curls put Shirley Temple's to shame. The red dress was perfect. "Oh, sweetheart, you look amazing," I said, entering the front door with a handful of carnations. Maggie's grin was absolutely enormous. "Your hair is perfect. And your dress is so beautiful." She couldn't contain her poise any longer, and she dashed into my arms. I didn't care that the flowers were being crushed. They would have to be content to be victims of a holy embrace. We were off.

After I buckled her seatbelt, I looked back at her

in the rearview mirror. Scratch that, I took a million pictures of her with my eyes. She looked too beautiful. So pure. She was beaming. "Oh, honey," I said as I turned to look at her. "I wasn't just talking about your hair and dress. I was also talking about your soul. Your personality. The way you think. You're so beautiful inside and out."

"I can't wait to grow up and marry you, Daddy," she responded. I loved absolutely every minute of this stage. If I could have frozen her in time, at that very moment, I honestly would have.

A strong wintery wind whistled over the car. Deep down, I knew the cold, harsh reality that someday Maggie would grow up. And it's my job to help her do just that. Now she wants to look pretty for her man — me. Years from now, it'll be Jimmy behind the cash register or Tony in her freshman college philosophy class.

"Oh, Lord, bless her knight in shining armor. He's out there. And You know him. As her father, I ask you to protect this boy who will grow up to be a man and ask for her hand in marriage. Keep him pure, Lord. Place a protective ring around his mind and soul. I know You can do this, Lord, and I thank You," I prayed aloud for Maggie to hear.

"There," I said. "Let's get moving. We've got some dancing to do!"

Reflections from Mom...

When our two oldest kids started school, we realized very quickly that they were going to hear things from other kids that we weren't ready for them to hear yet. And considering the sexual images and messages constantly bombarding us in our culture, we wanted to be proactive and get the right message to our kids before they heard the wrong one from somewhere else. But how to go about it?

I don't even really remember having "the birds and the bees" talk with my own parents, but I do know that I felt a certain amount of awkwardness and dread about broaching the subject with my own children.

Thank God, someone at a Christian marriage conference introduced us to a wonderful series called God's Design for Sex. There are four books geared toward different-age children. We began reading these with our children when they were very young.

The books really helped us explain God's divine design for a man and a woman: love, physical unity

in marriage, and the absolute marvel it is when a new life is created. The kids ate it up and had lots of questions. I realized that they had no embarrassment at all, which helped me get beyond my own and talk to them openly. I just prayed that they would continue to come to me with their questions.

That prayer was answered unexpectedly when I recently took Joseph in for his annual physical. After I filled out all the standard paperwork, the doctor handed Joseph a questionnaire, saying, "We don't want your mom to have to do all the work, so we'll have you fill this one out." Being the suspicious mom that I am, I sat down with Joe and read it with him.

It was a very explicit "sexual issues questionnaire." While waiting for the doctor to come back in, we talked over some of the questions. Much to my joy, Joseph was not familiar with a lot of the issues discussed. "What's that, Mom?" he asked a couple of times. I was thrilled that he showed no embarrassment about talking about any of it with me, and I said a silent prayer for the small but oh-so-important victory.

Legacy Letters

"The check arrived today, hon," my wife said as I placed my bag by the fridge. I loosened my tie. A long exhale sought to rid my body of the stress of the day. She handed me the envelope. It looked official. The return address confirmed the contents.

"What does 'esquire' mean, anyway?" I asked in a grumpy tone, knowing that I really didn't want to open it.

"What, dear?" my wife asked on her way to the dishwasher.

"Nothing," I mumbled, turning the envelope over in my hands.

The letter had been sent by a very diligent lawyer who had handled the matters of my grandmother's estate. The case was now officially settled. Done. I now knew that. All the beneficiaries had received a similar letter.

The contents contained a piece of her legacy. I thought of my grandmother, and something in my heart ached a bit. I sighed again. From across the room, my wife loved me with her tender smile.

I didn't know how long it had been since my grandmother had passed away. Eight months. Maybe ten. All I knew was that I wasn't ready for the letter. I was tempted to write "return to sender" on it. But I knew that would be just playing a silly game. With time and reality. Somehow, opening the envelope felt like officially closing the book on her life. The woman who had given me so much in her life was presenting me with one last gift. "Even after you're gone, Grammy, you just keep giving," I said softly.

I placed the envelope on the kitchen table. And there it sat. For three days.

Before your little heart floods with envy as you imagine how much money was inscribed on the estate check that patiently sat next to our salt-and-pepper shakers, let me tell you about Grammy. Actually, a proper introduction is in order. Her name was Genevieve. Isn't that such a beautiful name? When pronounced in French, it sounds melodious. When I became an adult, I would teasingly call my grandmother by her first name. She would always flash a mischievous smile when I did it. "Hi Genna," I'd say kiddingly while ushering my kids into her tidy family room. Her white hair was always perfectly cared for. Everything in her home was in order. Just like her estate. Long before that "esquire" gentleman came onto the scene, I was one of her beneficiaries — a fortunate recipient of Genevieve's love.

Her parents were of Polish descent, and at the ripe old age of twenty, she married a handsome man who was soon off to fight the German forces in World War II. They moved into a small home. Their American dream was under way. It was just blocks away from where she played hopscotch as a little girl. While Grandpa was overseas earning a purple heart, Grammy was home painting the nursery. She had a bun in the oven. And in that simple, three-bedroom, one-bath home, with a yard so small it took ten minutes to mow, Genevieve had her first daughter, Carol. My mom. That was the first of many gifts this sweet Polish woman bequeathed this author. When Grandpa came home, he peddled mail for the post office and tied grapes on the shores of Lake Erie. Their family grew, as did many in America when the veterans returned home to their beautiful, young wives.

"And now you know the rest of the story," Paul Harvey would poetically say into the microphone. Except you really don't. There are too many stories to tell. Some are knee-slapping funny. Others can make you cringe and even question your faith. There aren't enough authors out there to document the small and large memories that weave together a historic tapestry we call one's legacy.

A business associate of mine is a self-made millionaire.

His annual income is 1.7 million dollars. And it's growing. Not too shabby, eh? Yes, he has all the cars, watches, and experiences that money can buy. You and I lick our lips. "If only..." we begin. And yet if we confine our understanding of legacy to dollars, we're short-changing ourselves. One day, he said something to me that I found acutely profound. It was this: "The real measure of a man's wealth is his value if he lost all his money."

Those "esquire" types have to deal with legacy matters that involve assets, trusts, property, and the like. That's all well and good, but when it comes to legacy and your heritage, focusing on homes and bank accounts alone is far too shallow. That "stuff" just skims the surface. We need to look much deeper into what we leave behind. And what's been left behind to us. And that starts (not to be simplistic here) by how we live. And what we do with our time. Yes, this chapter isn't just about Grammy's legacy. It's about yours and mine as well.

As a parent who wants to raise terrific Christian kids, you are no doubt feeding your daughter's faith. You diligently safeguard your son's health and mind. Your daughter is afforded great opportunities and experiences. This life you are creating and providing can be wrapped up in one family quilt called "legacy." One day, your children will reminisce about how you made the perfect blueberry pie in the summertime ... and that you were a Scrabble wiz ... how you handled money ... that nobody could put the sheets on a bed like you ... and your laugh — well, nobody could forget how you hiccupped like crazy once you started laughing ... how you cried at every Hallmark commercial ... and that family RV trip.

The memories go on and on, don't they? Big ones and small ones blend together like ingredients for a magnificent stew, which stays warm in the crockpot of your mind.

Of course, your faith is perhaps the most prized gift you can leave behind. "What was his faith like?" a stranger could ask your children. "I ... I don't really know," some might say hesitantly. "She was kinda private with it, I guess. I know she believed in God and all that stuff, but ... " The answer fades away like a distant memory. Others might offer a different response: "His faith was everything. He loved the Lord. Like, really! And you could tell. He'd talk to God all the time. Whenever I struggled, my Dad would pray *with* me, not just about me. Man, his faith held our home together." I don't want to speak for you, but I sure hope my kids will be able to respond with the latter.

Let's roll up our sleeves...

TAKE STOCK. Before you take stock of your family tree, do yourself a favor. Grab a mug of coffee, sit down, and read 2 Kings: 21-23. It won't take long. The author chronicles the reigns of various kings. Now, if there was ever a person who could look on his family tree with utter disdain, it was King Josiah. Trust me on this. Talk about dysfunctional families. The British paparazzi and tabloids would have had a field day during this two-hundred-fifty-year period.

Let's take a quick peek at Josiah's family tree, shall we? The patriarch, Josiah's grandfather, is described in detail in chapter 21. King Manasseh's character is vividly portrayed. It isn't pretty. "He did evil in the sight of the Lord," verse 2 begins. "Ahem," Josiah clears his throat while flipping through the family photo album. "He built altars in the house of the Lord," verse 4 begins. "OK, not so bad," Josiah says in a hopeful tone. "Maybe Grandpa is redeeming himself here."

Try again. The altars were erected for false gods. Grandpa Manasseh then dutifully burnt his own son as an offering. Child sacrifice is a poor legacy, you know. So, too, is soothsaying and consulting with ghosts. The final nail in this dysfunctional king's coffin comes in verse 16: "Moreover, Manasseh did evil in the sight of the Lord, shedding so much innocent blood as to fill the length and breadth of Jerusalem." How'd you like that etched on your gravestone?

And Josiah's old man? He was arrogant and lazy. Second Kings didn't even spend one chapter on King Amon. To be exact, God's Word only found it worthwhile to spend seven sentences on the pitiful king. That's it. Josiah's dad mocked believers and sacred spaces. His reign lasted two whole years. When he was at the ripe old age of twenty-four, his friends had seen enough. King Amon was assassinated. Another legacy bites the dust.

Josiah's dear old Dad was now gone. Josiah was only eight. Our timeline now brings us to the throne of a pre-pubescent lad whose oversized crown rests awkwardly on his young head. "And … what happens next?" you ask. "Does the apple fall far from the tree?" you wonder. Patience, dear reader. We'll get back to our king in a minute.

Let's turn our attention to you and me for a brief moment. Josiah would like that. He already knows how his story plays out. Ours is still being written. How's your family tree? Some are ashamed of their past. Dan won't talk to his father to this very day. The memories are too painful. The arguments were too loud. Bridget walks this earth burdened with the wounds of abuse. Horrible things happened. You'd cringe if I told you. Or maybe you already know what it's like? Words were said with such venom that the poison still courses through her veins. "When I grow up," John says, wiping a resentful tear from his fourteen-year-old cheek, "I'll never be like Dad. He's pathetic."

Hopefully your family tree isn't as gloomy as Josiah's. Or as others' you may know. Either way, you gotta take stock. Josiah did. Now you have a little kingdom of your own — a small tribe parading around in diapers, perhaps. Or maybe a mob of teenagers eating you out of house and home. Regardless, it's your time to take note of the legacy that you were left with. Look over your shoulder and take everything that hurt, shattered, or cursed and discard it. And I mean all of it. Throw it away. It's worthless, useless garbage. Then hold on to anything that worked — the encouragement, blessings, discipline, praise, wisdom, and love, and run with 'em! It's time to take action. Grab a pen. Let's write a legacy for yourself that would make King Josiah proud.

TAKE ACTION. Josiah must have felt some pressure from the masses when he sat on the throne for the first time. Do you think he heard their suspicious whispers? "He looks just like his dirty, rotten father," some might have hissed. "Yeah, and I bet he's as bloodthirsty as his grandpa," another voice probably murmured in the darkness. If anyone had the right to play victim and use his storied past as an excuse to live wildly, it was Josiah. His role models stunk. His family tree was decaying. The future didn't look so bright.

And yet Josiah broke the chain. At some key point in his young reign, Josiah drew a line in the sand. "No more!" I can see him stating emphatically. "This is my ship now, and I'm charting a new course." And that he did.

How about you? Where's your ship headed? If you truly want to leave an impressive legacy, then you'll need to follow our young king's lead.

❖ **Banish addictions and habitual sin from your kingdom!** Just open your Bible to 2 Chronicles and take a look at what Josiah did once he took the royal office. He issued an all-out assault on the false gods of the time. Altars to these popular, bogus gods were dismantled. Destroyed. On purpose. "Not in my house!" Josiah exclaimed as the putrid altars crumbled to the ground.

Regardless of where we've come from, who we've been with, and what we've experienced, there comes a pivotal moment in our lives when we must destroy the altars erected in our wounded hearts. The altars of our addictions and habitual sins promise fulfillment and peace. We go to them often. Daily. Religiously. Far too much incense has been burned at their thick, granite bases. These false gods — for that is what they truly are, dear reader — enchant us with a counterfeit spell. One that leaves us craving for more. We receive but are never satisfied. The truth is, we walk away from these altars feeling empty, ashamed, and hollow, only to return the next day for more. It's tragic.

Just as blue eyes and auburn hair are passed on from one generation to the next, so, too, are addictions and habitual sins. "I can't believe I'm struggling with alcohol," one despondent friend said to me. "I swore I'd never touch the stuff!" Her sunken eyes beckoned for liberation. And hope. "My Grandpa used to pass out on the kitchen floor. And

my Dad just drank himself to sleep every night. Ah!
I hate what it's done to my family!" Her voice
became faint. This thirty-one-year-old mother
whimpered: "I hate who I've become!"

It's time to "pull a Josiah," I said. "With God's grace,
you can break the chain of slavery. The time is now.
Hurry — your legacy hasn't been fully written yet.
Josiah did it and so can you. Banish this false god
from your family tree. Years from now, your kids
and grandkids will thank you for being the one who
put an end to it — for good."

> Forgive us the wrongs we have done, as we
> have forgiven those who have wronged us.
>
> MATTHEW 6:12 (REB)

❖ **Destroy the altar of unforgiveness.** I've spent
   more time with you in this chapter than all the
   others. There's a method to my madness. Your
   legacy cannot be taken lightly. Some day an
   author might just write about your life, putting
   your imprint on the seashore of time. Like they
   wrote about King Manasseh and his son Amon.
   And like the way they wrote about the gutsy
   Josiah. Your legacy is of great consequence.
   It's everything.

So walk with me for a moment. Come on. I gotta show you something. We pass the dismantled altars of addictions and habitual sins as we solemnly walk through a large corridor. It's illuminated by torches. You notice the walls are covered with thousands upon thousands of pictures. Each photo is placed in its own little frame. Amazed at this vast collection, you pause. You're curious.

And then you notice that each picture represents a moment in your life. You take one frame off the wall. You look. "I was twenty-four in this one," you comment. "My wedding," you say fondly and then smash the frame on the ground. "I can't believe my dad didn't come to my big day!" You grab hold of another. "Oh, my... look," you speak to the dark air in the chamber. "It's my fifth grade picture. I had the worst bowl cut ever," you say, giggling. "That was the year my body started to change, and my brother teased me. Ruthlessly."

"Where am I?" you ask. You sprint forward, past the last of the torches, into a large gold chamber. And there you stand. At the base of the biggest altar you've ever seen. And upon it is the false god of unforgiveness.

This twisted deity promises healing and resolution if you relive your pain just one more time. "Harbor that hurt," it pleads seductively. "Keep thinking about it. And talking about it. Never let that painful memory die! Hold onto it with all your heart. It's your right to remember how you were wronged," a voice speaks from the darkness. And sadly, we do just that. With each resentment anchored securely in your soul's harbor, your heart becomes suspicious, distrusting, and callous. Over time the memories become like fossils, embedded in stone.

God's love has a terrible time finding its way through the granite of unforgiveness that now encases your heart. Tomb-like. Yes, this altar must go. Now! If no action is taken, your heart, ever so slowly, becomes imprisoned in a dark chamber of pain. And far worse than even your sorry plight, is the legacy of unforgiveness you leave for the next generation.

Please, don't just take my word for it. I'm just a forty-year-old dad who's messed up in this area more times than he cares to admit. Again, go to the Source. See what the Prince of Peace has to say about forgiveness. I think we'd agree that He found it mighty important. Better yet, pray His prayer with me. And when you get to the "forgive us our trespasses" part, I double dare ya to mean it.

❖ **Create a Legacy Binder.** Next to the laptop into which I feverishly type sits a basic, black binder.

But between the ordinary, scuffed covers are crammed pages of extraordinary tales. You see, it's my legacy binder. Let me explain. When something unique, sacred, or downright silly happens in our wonderful home, I seize the opportunity to write about it. Like the aspiring reporter fresh out of college, I always have a small notepad nearby.

Each page in this binder is a legacy letter written to one of my kids. "Dear Joe," I begin my letter and then proceed to write about a moment he and I shared in this grand adventure called life. With some, I attach photographs (like the time Maggie and I went to our first father-daughter dance). To others I attach appropriate memorabilia (like a ticket stub from a Yankees game or a hospital bracelet from the ER). Get my drift?

What I'm trying to communicate in the letter is that I "noticed" my son or daughter. I was aware of their life. And I was in it with them. And so, in each documentation, I want them to hear my gratitude and awe. For them and for the One who gave us each other. When they are adults with families of their own, I hope my simple letters provide them with the assurance that their father loves them. And that their Father in heaven loves them even more.

TAKE TIME TO PRAY. Josiah did. Actually, if we turn our gaze back to him in 2 Kings: chapter 22, we see that he did much more than sit quietly in a pew. Scripture tells us that this wise king humbled himself before the Lord. He wept in contrition for the sins of his forefathers and his people. The whole kingdom had turned its back on God. And yet the prayers of one man — one righteous man — brought God's favor on the land.

ROLL UP YOUR SLEEVES RESOURCES

- *Your Best Life Now,* by Joel Osteen
- *Breaking Free,* by Beth Moore
- *Be A Man,* by Fr. Larry Richards

Perhaps it's time to weep for the past. To finally seek God's healing so that altars can be dismantled and hearts restored. Like the young mother who "hated who she had become," perhaps you, too, look into the mirror with shame. Don't forget — Josiah's God is your God, too. Our Father loves to breathe new life into our souls. To restore. To make new. That's what He does. All the time.

Surrender. That's the word for this section. Put your arms straight up in the air and call out, "I give up!" Place the chains of addiction and habitual sin on the cross. They need to die. And all those photographs of resentment and pain — bring them, too. Jesus knew all about surrender. He freely stretched his arms out wide, surrendering to the Father's divine plan. Surrendering to the nails, so that you and I could be free.

My favorite line in the entire story of Josiah can be easily skipped over. It causes us to focus on our old friend David. Remember this great king we talked about in chapter six? Apparently Josiah was determined to look back in his family history and find someone to emulate. "There must have been a good apple somewhere," I imagine he prayed. When he got to King David, he stopped his search. Here was finally a man, certainly an imperfect man, but one who sought to live an honorable and virtuous life.

The author of 2 Kings 22:2 writes: "He did what was right in the eyes of the Lord, following in the footsteps of his forefather David and deviating neither to the right nor to the left"(REB)." Pray that someday, when your legacy is remembered, your children may write the same about you.

Not long ago, two of my boys were having a special indoor campout in the living room. Popcorn. *Star Wars* for the eightieth time. The works! They scrambled for their favorite blankets. That's half the fun of sleeping on the couch, you know. Gus got the best blanket. Thirty-three years ago my mom had quilted it. I remember watching her patiently cut patterns, arrange them just so, and assemble her masterpiece. I was seven. Little did I know at that time that she was going to be with me only five more short years.

She was so proud of her quilt. So much so that it hung on our living-room wall. For years. Even after she was gone. I always thought of it as a type of banner in honor of Mom. When Dad was selling the house, he offered it to my wife and me. It was an honor to bring her quilt home. It brought back many special memories. And now, this symbolic piece of her legacy was enveloping my son as he slept. He looked so peaceful in the quilt made by the Grandma he had never had the chance to know. "Nice quilt, Mom," I said looking up to heaven after kissing my boy. I winked. "I mean Grandma."

The house was quiet and still. It was time. I walked to the kitchen and grabbed the envelope. The letter was half-colored by artistic, Crayola-filled hands. The backside had spaghetti-sauce spots all over it. "Poor little guy," I said to the envelope. "You got yourself a bad case of pasta acne."

I broke the seal and removed the letter that symbolized Grammy's legacy. I held the check.

No, I didn't place it in a briefcase handcuffed to my wrist and rush off to a Swiss Bank. I don't think they're interested in deposits just over $3,000. Instead, that money sits in an online savings account, waiting for just the right time to make a strategic withdrawal and reinvest that money into the next generation. "Who knows, maybe it'll fund a trip to Poland," I mused. "Yeah, Grammy would like that." I smiled thinking of all the legacy letters I'd write out of that pilgrimage. Or maybe we can buy some great fabric and knit ourselves a fabulous family quilt. "Not a bad idea," I surmised.

Oh, God, help me to live an amazing life. One that gives You glory and leaves a legacy so significant that my kids, grandkids, and their kids can wrap themselves in my memory and be instructed, inspired, and blessed. Amen.

Reflections from Dad...

This is a sample of an actual letter I have in my Legacy Binder.

Dear Joe,

This week you and I crossed another major father-son milestone in our lives. Together we ventured off to conquer new land. No, we didn't sail down the rocky coast. Or find a hidden path in a state park and traverse up a steep cliff. But we did do something just as adventurous and fun — we hit the links!

It's hard to describe what went through my mind and heart as we approached the first tee. There's something (dare I say sacred) about a father and son golfing for the first time. Now, I won't go as far as to compare it to the unique initiation ceremonies that you find in remote tribal societies; however, I do hold that there is a special initiation element to it.

You see, Joe, I didn't just take you out on the golf course for a quick round. I took you out into the world. That's my job. We left home — together — and went somewhere exciting. I took you to a place where you would discover new vistas. I took you somewhere where the biggest challenge would be yourself. How do you handle an errant shot into the pond? Or a great shot, for that matter? Would you get down on yourself for a poor play, or would you be able to enjoy the game even if you weren't perfect? Would you fudge your score when it was time to be accountable for the hole or shoot straight with me? Would you be so focused on your game that you missed opportunities to enjoy the view and the great shots made by your playing partner? These are just a sampling of the questions I had in my mind when you slapped your first drive onto the fairway.

The golf course is a great testing ground of one's true character. We practiced a lot in the backyard. You took lessons. But on the course it's just you and that little, white ball. How you play the game depends on your skill, attitude, and integrity.

The world is pretty much the same way, Joe. Someday you'll leave home and start a life of your own. Hopefully, Mom and I have equipped you with the spiritual, emotional, intellectual, and moral skills to "play well" in your life.

When you and I met on the golf course, every cell in my body longed for you to succeed and enjoy the game. I rejoiced in your great shots and sympathized with you when I saw you struggling in the sand trap. Through the good and the ugly, I was with you on that course. For every shot. Rooting my boy on to victory. And regardless of the score represented on the card attached to this note, I was proud of you from the first hole to the last. You're my son. I'll be with you for your whole life through.

Love,
Dad

Reflections from Mom...

My son's baseball game was almost over, and I was more than ready to get home and get dinner on the stove. But I had thoroughly enjoyed the casual conversations with the other parents throughout the game. One gentleman had asked where I was from. When I told him my hometown and my maiden name, he asked if I was related to Art Flynn. "Yes," I replied with a sense of fondness. "He was my uncle."

The man smiled and said, "He was such a good man, that Art. One of the best."

"Yes, he was," I agreed.

As the game ended and I walked to my car, I found myself thinking of my uncle, who had passed away when I was just seventeen. This wasn't the first time someone had made such a comment. From time to time, at random moments, the same type of conversation would occur. And every single time the individual would speak of my late uncle with a deep sense of respect.

The victim of a massive heart attack, my uncle had passed away at the young age of forty-five, leaving his wife and two grown children, my cousins. To say the whole family and community was bereft with shock and grief would be an understatement. His loss was felt by many.

Now, twenty years later, I found myself missing him. I remembered the summer they lived with us temporarily while they looked for a permanent home. One of my favorite memories of him was one evening when he offered to comb through the tangles in my freshly shampooed hair. I will never forget how gently he worked through all the knots, talking and joking around with me the whole time, as if, at that moment, I was the center of his universe.

As I arrived home and tended to the mundane task of cooking yet another meal, this cherished memory brought a fresh perspective that from the simple, ordinary things of life can come a great legacy, especially when done with great love.

"Thanks for reminding me of that, Uncle Art," I said with a smile as I called the kids for dinner.

As For You and Your House?

Just imagine wandering around the desert for forty years. Seriously. I'm forty and can't even put my arms around that time frame. All that time, just wandering, foraging for food, seeking shelter in the rain. Looking for a place to call home.

It must have been something when the Israelites finally got settled. No more "hoping" the Promised Land would be around the next bend. No more living like a small circus contingent, constantly packing and unpacking. And no more impatient little voices asking Moses from the back of the caravan, "Are we there yet?" You thought your last family trip wore you out!

Now try to imagine what it must have been like when the forty-year trek was finally over. Talk about an excuse for a party. But wedged between the long hike and celebration — like sweet Oreo filling — we find Joshua.

Joshua valiantly served as commander-in-chief after Moses died. He was God's handpicked leader. His mission was straightforward: mobilize the troops, fight battles against a lot of guys whose last names end in "-ites," and claim the Promised Land. The time had finally come. Enough walking already. Everyone could see the light at the end of the tunnel.

Joshua's military victories were unique and swift, to say the least. He'd be the first to admit that it always helps to have "the Big General upstairs" drafting the battle plans. Phase one was complete. "Mission accomplished," Joshua humbly called out to God. It was now time to claim the land his people had sought for oh so long.

And yet, before Joshua bellowed, "Let's move 'em out … we're goin' home, boys!" he paused. No, he wasn't looking for the chilled champagne and party hats. He wasn't fishing in his backpack for his video recorder so he could post a clip on Facebook. You see, he had a challenge for the group. Hidden within it was a probing question. I call it "the question." The kind that pins you against a wall until you give your answer. Here it is:

> If it does not please you to serve the Lord, decide today whom you will serve …
>
> JOSHUA 24:15

Of course, we all know what comes right after that. It's that all-too-familiar, bold declaration that has made its way to the elegant canvas of Christian artists as well as calendars and coffee mugs. Songs have been written on these famous words from our dear friend Joshua. He fearlessly shouted for all the world to hear:

As for me and my household, we will serve the Lord!

I first chuckled when I read this passage. "Are you kidding me, Joshua?" I asked aloud. "You guys were lost. Aimless. On the move for more than forty years! Yet God was there for you every step of the way. Who *wouldn't* serve the Lord? He's the One who saw you folks through — despite all of your hard-heartedness and stubbornness!"

Think about it. They wondered out loud if the grass was greener in Egypt. "We can go back and be Pharaoh's slaves," some grumbled. God didn't hold a grudge that they had already forgotten the events at the Red Sea. Remember that whole golden calf episode? Yeah, while they were parading around with "Goldie the Wonder Cow," God had some one-on-one time with Moses. He wasn't plotting revenge. Or whom to thunderbolt first. No, our Wonderful Counselor was fixing to provide this unruly mob with ten divine instructions that would serve as a spiritual roadmap for their lost souls. And ours. How about the time these folks complained about no food? They hadn't seen a McDonald's for days. Their bellies ached and their tongues whined. God responded with food literally sent down from heaven.

At every miscalculated turn, He was there with a divine road sign. After every act of disobedience, He offered mercy. When they complained, nitpicked, and fought amongst themselves, he offered words of wisdom and peace. When they sat arms crossed, mouths open wide, screaming like a baby locked in a highchair, he spoon-fed 'em. And when the bad guys circled their camp like a ravenous pack of wolves? He rolled up His sleeves and provided the big guns.

The list goes on and on here. See why I was so amazed that Joshua made the statement with the implied question? Even better — why would he even have to? Simple, really. Unlike God, we tend to forget. Joshua had to ask, because he knew how his gang thought: "The Red Sea, manna, stone tablets, battle support ... yeah, that's all great, but that was last week ... last month, and last year! I'm worried about now!"

Joshua knew their memories were short. "Today they're murmuring about something," I could just hear him say. "And then they're happy, and before you blink, they're wondering why God has abandoned them again. Ah!" So he made a statement that posed "the question": "Are you in, or out? Is God your God forever, or not?"

I f it does not please you to serve the Lord, decide today whom you will serve ...

JOSHUA 24:15

Don't forget now, this Bible of ours is timeless. It has no shelf life. No expiration date. No recalls. The question Joshua asked his companions is a pretty good one for you and me, too. "But life is so different now," you might say. Is it? Yeah, our Adidas sandals are certainly more comfortable than those stiff, flat, leather ones Moses wore back in the day. And our mode of transportation has certainly evolved from the compact mule. Yet we humans haven't changed all that much. Joshua's indirect question asks us to take stock, to remember God's blessings. Because ... well ... we forget.

My wife and I diligently prayed for a healthy baby. We got one, and then we moaned about sleep deprivation and our martyr-like sacrifice of getting up at three o'clock in the morning. I asked God for help and guidance through the toddler years and in the same breath pleaded for the "terrible twos" to pass in warp speed. I thanked Him for my son's growth and development, yet grumbled in my prayers about the pains of having a teenager. We prayed for kids, yet often cuddled and nurtured self-pity for all the trials and tribulations that come with having them. Come on now, I'm not the only one who seems to forget God's blessings, am I?

Parenthood is no walk in the park. You and I know that. It's probably more like a forty-year quest through unknown valleys, thick swamplands, and impassable mountain peaks. Yet, despite our pleadings, grumblings, and forgetfulness, God is there directing our paths.

The day this chapter was written, our family had read a small section of chapter 24 in Joshua. I won't even try to impress you here with this true story. Prayer was pretty chaotic. It was terribly humid and our old air conditioner was humming furiously. One of my boys had been cranky all day, and two others were bouncing off the walls. I had a pounding headache. "All right, folks, gather 'round," I yelled over the laboring AC. I knew that a ten-minute prayer was all that the family could handle at present.

My daughter read from the Word of God. I then talked to the kids about "the question." Kinda like I just talked to you, but more kid-like. "These people were lost and God just kept helping them. He gave them food. And military support." (One of my younger boys perked up his ears and even set down his GI Joe when he heard that one.) "Then He brought them to this awesome place. And this Joshua guy — their leader — had to ask everyone a really important question before they started building houses and stuff ..."

Then it hit me. No, not the block my rambunctious three-year-old had just hurled into the Freon-filled air. That hit his grumpy brother, which I could tell didn't contribute to his present mood. Right then and there, in the midst of a very imperfect family prayer, I realized that Joshua had demanded an answer to his question. *My* answer.

"Yeah," I said aloud in front of my wife and kids. "We will serve the Lord." Everyone just looked at me. It was awkward for a moment. But that didn't last long. My wife picked up on it pretty quickly. "Yes. We will serve the Lord," she said with her beautiful smile. Then we went around the room. Everyone was asked the question. And everyone was asked to respond. And each member of the family did. We were united. It was absolutely awesome!

The answer to this key biblical question sets the foundation for raising terrific Christian kids, to be sure. There are no books, counselors, seminars, or websites that compare with the grace and assistance that flows from a faithful and all-knowing Father. Who, by the way, also wants you to raise terrific Christian kids. Think about it. The answer to this "question" provides hope, perspective, and direction in almost any situation. Let's take a quick stroll through this book:

Chapter 1: Be Madly in Love With Your Spouse

Your marriage has kinda been put on the back burner. It's been a month or two since you and your spouse have been on a date. Or even really talked, for that matter! Take hold of her hand and answer "the question." Together. Breathe. Regroup and go grab a bite to eat.

Chapter 2: Teach Blessing

You've been caught up with deadlines at work and shuttling kids to soccer and Scouts. Feeling overextended, you secretly wonder if you'll ever get it all done. Then you realize it's been weeks since you placed your hand on your son's head and blessed him. You know it's what he secretly longs for. Kneel by his bedside and answer "the question." Then bless your boy.

Chapter 3: Sometimes Less is More

While trying to figure out even the most basic of features on your new smartphone (like how to dial a phone number), you realize that you've spent almost no time today praying with your spouse and for your kids. "Put the phone down, mister. Slowly. I got my eyes on you," your conscience whispers to your soul in police-like fashion. "Hurry up and get on your knees." Don't even know how to begin praying, Mr. Techno-Gadget? How about starting with answering "the question"? Then take it from there.

Chapter 4: I Love Your Life!

You bubble over with excitement knowing that you got the last Tickle Me Elmo doll in the county. While wrapping her gifts, you realize this birthday celebration might have gone way overboard. There were gifts aplenty, but perspective on the day was lacking. It's OK to be excited and want to make the day special, but deep down, you know it's time to answer "the question."

Chapter 5: Bite Your Tongue!

"4:29!" someone shouts emphatically while pointing an accusatory finger at your guilty face. Most of the time it's funny, but not today. Your tirade on your boss and crazy co-worker is more than justified. But you know your daughter's right. Even though you had a crummy day at work, you just blew it with your mouth. Again. Where to start? Answer "the question" and pray your 3 Rs (*repent*, *replace*, and *revoke* all negative words said).

Chapter 6: Purity Ring

Everybody talked about the hot new movie. It was a box-office smash. So when you had the chance to check it out during a lull on your business trip, it was a no-brainer. That is, until twenty minutes into the film. Your eyes were downloading images that were anything but pure. You'd never let your kids watch this, but … "the question" interrupts your rationalization. "As for me and my house …" you begin to say as you exit the movie theater.

Chapter 7: Legacy Letters

You find yourself feeling anxious as you peer at your low 401k balance on the computer screen. "Bob retired when he was fifty-five," you think to yourself as you fret about your financial future. And then it hits you like a two-by-four across the side of your head. "I've spent more time worrying about retirement than I've spent creating a legacy for my kids." You turn the computer off, answer "the question," and set out to live a life worth imitating.

Your child just acted up, and you've reached your limit. He talked back to you in a disrespectful tone. She's sick of the rules. You and he keep butting heads. A less-than-favorable report card is thrown into the mix. You're angry. Frustrated. Overwhelmed. Guess what? Your kid is, too. How about the two of you sit down? And, you guessed it, answer "the question." Together. Out loud. Then, seek Him. Trust me on this. God can handle report cards, over-worked parents, disagreements, and, yes, even teenagers.

I can't help but wonder if that was the only time Joshua asked the implied question to the gang. I'll let biblical scholars wrestle with that one. Here's one thing I do know — it's a question, *the* question that my wife, children, and I need to answer. Every day.

And how about you, dear reader? You've been most generous to walk with me through these storied pages. I pray our time together hasn't felt like a forty-year odyssey in the desert. Since the wisest of all men are known by the quality of their questions, allow me to offer you one as we say goodbye. Don't worry; this is not the type of hopeless question a game-show host would throw at you for the ten-million-dollar prize. No need for lifelines here. It's not some philosophical question that the likes of Descartes and other great minds failed to answer. No, this one is basic. Fundamental. Your response is either Yes or No. Ready? Great, because Joshua and I just can't stand the suspense:

As for you and your household, will you serve the Lord?

Sittin' in a Catholic Pew

I love oatmeal. For sure it's on my top 10 comfort foods list. It's so easy to prepare and yet has that homemade quality that makes it rise above a bowl of some fortified flakes that grew stale in a box. Plus, you gotta admit that the guy on the front of the container looks so cool. Anyway, this last chapter was penned sitting at the kitchen table with a pipin' hot bowl of my favorite breakfast delicacy.

Forgive me for a moment while I sprinkle on some brown sugar. My oatmeal just wouldn't be complete without it. In the same way, Catholicism completes my Christian identity. And so, before I say "so long," I want to sprinkle my Catholic perspective on this book — to give you a taste of the view from a Catholic pew.

I wish I could show you my family album, because it's busting at the seams with photographs showing how my

Catholic identity has been with me from a very young age. You'd chuckle at the "bowl cut" I sported the day of my first Communion. My mom was so happy that day and, even though she has since passed away, I can still recall her talking to me about what a big step it was in my faith.

Besides my mom, nobody impacted my faith more than my grandparents. They were old-school Catholics who would share with me mysterious traditions like what it was like to attend a Latin Mass. My Polish grandfather was a giant to me. He was a World War II veteran decorated with the Purple Heart, but that's not what impressed me most. It was his quiet faith. He loved to till the garden praying his rosary in a blend of Polish and English, and I fondly recall trying to keep up while not stepping on the strawberry plants.

And then there's Nanny, my paternal grandmother. Even though she was no more than 5'2" (with heels), her life was such an incredible pillar of Catholic faith for me. My brother and I would always spend our Easter vacation at Nanny's house, and she made sure we had tons of fun. But she also kept our young eyes focused on the richness of the liturgical season. Fridays in Lent consisted of two simple meals, and piling into the car for 3 o'clock confessions.

Since I am a cradle Catholic, my world has always been permeated with these beautiful prayers and rituals, and the more I have come to understand them and try to live them the more they have enriched my life. I love being Catholic, I love the sacraments of the Church, and I love sharing the traditions and treasures of the faith with my kids and friends. But where to start? Let's head to the back of the church where an amazing sacrament of mercy takes place — in the confessional.

Confession — Man, I have 1,000 great confession stories for you (oh, yeah, I need to go a lot!), but one particularly comes to mind. Now, I won't waste your time by telling you all that I did or didn't do to get to that confessional kneeler. That's not my main point here. But I will call your attention to the metallic, creaking sound of the door as I stepped into the main foyer of the church. You know the sound. Those rusty hinges needed attention. And so did my soul.

I walked into this sacrament feeling pretty corroded. I had been overworked, overstressed, and downright disgusted with my sin. As I confessed my sins, the priest sometimes seemed to be lost in prayer. At other times he would stop to ask a question, or offer an understanding nod. There was no judgment in his eyes. Just compassion. He listened. Patiently. He offered counsel, directed me to key scripture passages, and reminded me of the faith that I profess. And then, absolution. Such a great word. Such a great gift.

It was a simple, ordinary confessional experience, and yet when I re-entered the world via that same rusty door, I felt extraordinary. Clean. Forgiven. Restored. New. Like a well-oiled spiritual machine. Confession puts everything in its right place. I am a sinner. I've given my heart and soul to Christ, but I'm still a man battling my pride and sinfulness. God is the forgiver, and the healer of my soul. I must repent of my sins, confess them, resolve to live in virtue, avoid occasions of sin, and then, through the action of the priest, receive the forgiveness and grace of Christ — which makes all things new. This gift cannot be earned, and it is not some type of spiritual reward because I have gold stars on my soul.

ROLL UP YOUR SLEEVES RESOURCES

- *Lord, Have Mercy: The Healing Power of Confession,* by Scott Hahn.
- *Pardon and Peace: A Sinner's Guide to Confession,* by Fr. Francis Randolph
- *How to Make a Good Confession,* by John A. Kane
- *Go in Peace,* by Fr. Mitch Pacwa

Like the father in the prodigal son parable, God just can't wait to embrace our battered and wounded souls.

It's hard for me to admit my sins. To the man in the mirror. To God. And sometimes to a trusted priest. But one thing comes to mind that I always say to my kids — sometimes the best things in life are the hardest things in life. Walk with me for a minute into the pages of the Bible. Let me set the stage. Jesus was about to appear to his apostles after His resurrection. Yet the very ones who were closest to Christ were hiding from the world behind a locked door. They were afraid. Christ entered the room, breathed on them, and spoke these empowering words:

R eceive the Holy Spirit. Whose sins you forgive are forgiven them, and whose sins you retain are retained.

JOHN 20:22-23

Now I'm no Bible scholar, but I'm guessing He thought this confession thing was pretty important if He was giving His imperfect apostles the authority to forgive sin in His name. It's amazing … when you and I kneel in the confessional and repent of our sins, we are truly whispering in the ear of Christ. It's Christ, Himself, who meets us in the confessional in the person of the priest. As He revealed to a simple, Polish nun, St. Faustina (one of my favorite saints):

> *When you approach the confessional, know this, that I Myself am waiting there for you. I am only hidden by the priest, but I Myself act in your soul* (Diary, 1602).

I'll never forget the first time my son went to confession. It was truly a liberating experience for me. Not just because he was beginning to repent of his sins on his own, but because it reminded me that I'm not his god. Jesus

Christ died and rose again for my kids and He longs to receive them in Heaven. He loves them far more than I do. I can forgive my son if he wrongs me, yes, but I cannot cleanse his soul. Only the Father who is rich in mercy can heal and restore. I can strive to be holy, and to form my son in the faith, but in the end, I can only point to the Savior who brings everlasting life.

Our kids will never beg us to take them to the dentist, or the doctor for a physical, and they're probably not going to pester us to take them to the confessional either. That's on you and me. We're the parents. I rarely miss changing the oil in my car after 3,000 miles, and yet I can go way too long before my knees bend in humility before the One who died for my sins. Am I the only one here, or did I just here an "amen" from someone sittin' in another Catholic pew?

So don't make this a huge production; just look at your calendar and pencil it in. Consider it routine soul maintenance. Go as a family. Lead your kids to the forgiving arms of Christ.

TAKE STOCK

When did I make my last confession? _____
How about my kids?_____

Do I help my kids prepare beforehand to receive all the grace that's available through this cleansing and healing sacrament? ☐ Yes or ☐ No

Have I made sure my kids understand the role of the priest in the confessional? ☐ Yes or ☐ No

When am I going to make my next confession?
_____ (Get your day planner out.)

The Eucharist — I'll never forget one Sunday when I hoisted up my two-year-old, Genevieve, to carry her towards the front of the church. It was time to receive the Eucharist and, quite honestly, it felt great to stand. It was a terribly humid day, and my shirt was saturated with sweat. The heat from my daughter's body caused my temperature to rise, and a bead of sweat cascaded from my forehead onto her summer dress.

I was tired and, as my wife so eloquently put it, a tad grumpy. As we processed down the main aisle, Genevieve whispered into my ear, "I want some, Daddy. I want some." I was too busy trying to keep my glasses from sliding off my sweaty nose to even acknowledge her comment, so she pressed on: "I want some, Daddy."

"Some of what?" I asked impatiently.

Her blue eyes grabbed my distracted spirit. "Some of Jesus, Daddy. Some of Him!" She pointed to the members of the congregation receiving the Eucharist.

At that moment, I realized how self-preoccupied I was. It was pathetic, actually. My two-year-old had just executed a spiritual body slam on me. As I lay on the mat, I asked myself: *Do you really want to receive Jesus, Jason? Are you fully into this, or just going through the motions? Are you approaching the King of Kings with child-like faith, or stuck in pride believing you can handle all your problems on your own? Why are you in church thinking about you instead of Him? Jesus is here, right now, in person, offering you His whole being! Where are you?* The *Catechism of the Catholic Church* states clearly that the Eucharist is the source and summit of our faith. Translation for us ordinary folk sittin' in the pews — the Eucharist is a pretty big deal.

*U*nless you eat the flesh of the Son of Man and drink his blood, you do not have life within you. Whoever eats my flesh and drinks my blood has eternal life, and I will raise him on the last day.

JOHN 6:52-54

Listen, I know that there will be some days that it's hard to fully put your heart into Mass, prayer, or what have you. I know that life can be taxing and that sometimes you feel like you're just running on empty. But the irony of it all is that we sometimes miss that the Eucharist was given to us to be our fuel. I like to view Mass as my opportunity to top off my spiritual tank.

> Whoever eats my flesh and drinks my blood remains in me and I in him. Just as the living Father sent me and I have life because of the Father, so also the one who feeds on me will have life because of me.
>
> JOHN 6:56-57

The Eucharist unites us with all of Heaven. It's our link to the One with whom we truly belong. It sometimes feels like I need a miracle greater than the parting of the Red Sea, though, to get my kids dressed and into the car so we can get to church on time. Trust me, there have been moments when I've acted more like a crazed drill sergeant than a loving shepherd trying to get our family to Mass. Just bein' honest here. But regardless of my imperfections, one truth I cling to is that my children have a whole lot better chance of being terrific Catholic kids if I bring them to the source and summit of their faith on a regular basis.

I just have to tell you about what I think is one of the best-kept secrets of the Catholic Church. You curious?

Daily Mass. Making the effort to fit Mass in your hectic schedule (even if it's once or twice a week) will provide you with a spiritual payout better than any jackpot. Especially when your spouse and kids are sittin' in the pew with ya.

ROLL UP YOUR SLEEVES RESOURCES

- *7 Secrets of the Eucharist,* by Vinny Flynn
- *The Lamb's Supper: The Mass as Heaven on Earth,* by Scott Hahn
- *In the Presence of Our Lord: The History, Theology, and Psychology of Eucharistic Devotion,* by Fr. Benedict Groeschel

Another way I try to impress upon my kids the great beauty of the Eucharist is by giving each of them "a turn" to come with me to our church's adoration chapel. I kinda look at it as a divine appointment. It's so refreshing to bring my kids before the King of Kings and allow them to bask in His presence. While in the small chapel, we find some time to read a scripture passage together, and maybe a kid's book about a popular saint. And then we pray. Together. In the presence of the One who created our souls and knows our needs before we even utter them.

TAKE STOCK

For the most part, do I simply go to Mass
out of a sense of obligation? ☐ Yes or ☐ No

Do I approach the Eucharist with my whole heart?
☐ Yes or ☐ No

Can I set aside some time in my schedule this week
to adore the Lord in the Eucharist?
☐ Yes or ☐ No
If so, when can I do that this week? _____
Whom should I bring along? _____

Have I recently talked to my kids about why we
genuflect, and the importance of the Eucharist in
their faith? ☐ Yes or ☐ No

Family Prayer — One of my spiritual heroes, an eighty-year-old Jesuit priest, never fails to say goodbye without throwing in his personal maxim. "Take time to pray," he'll say with a twinkle in his eye. Sounds so simple doesn't it? Allow me to add just three words to that short sentence, OK? Here it goes: "Take time to pray, as a family."

The other day someone mentioned that Grandpa was having a tough day. You know the kind. A thousand items on the "to-do list" and barely enough time to sharpen the pencil. Sound familiar? We couldn't do anything concrete and practical to assist him, but there was one thing we could do. Pray. As a family. And that's exactly what we did.

In the midst of a family room cluttered with Lego pieces, GI Joes, and baby dolls we gathered. In His name. We were on a mission. It was time to pray for the man our kids have been around ever since they could remember. They've grown up around their Grandfather (whom they affectionately call "Boppa") and have been richly blessed by him. So now it was their chance to lift him up with their heartfelt prayers. I'm struggling to describe it, but there's something so sacred about a family assembling to pray for a loved one. It just feels so much more effective than simply walking around being concerned. Make sense?

One of our favorite prayers is the rosary. It's one of the most biblical prayers we pray. The rosary is like a time machine that drops us smack dab in the middle of key Gospel moments (i.e., the Nativity, the Agony in the Garden, the Descent of the Holy Spirit on the Apostles). With eight kids, you can imagine that our family rosary doesn't always flow smoothly. Family prayer sometimes mirrors real life — it can be messy, disjointed, and full of distractions. But the beauty of this traditional Catholic prayer is that each mystery of the rosary gently brings our hearts and minds back into the presence of God.

Before I leave the topic of prayer, I just gotta talk about one more thing — gratitude. I've never met an unhappy grateful person. Think about it. Those two adjectives just don't go together. One of the ways we've tried to instill an attitude of gratitude in our home is by saying grace before each meal. Now it's not always natural to pause and pray, especially when your stomach's grumbling and there's a steaming plate of Mom's special dish under your nose. But it's in those moments when our appetites are clamoring for attention that our spiritual character is strengthened by the simple exercise of offering thanks to the Father.

And it's so basic, really. After making the sign of the cross (a really powerful prayer in itself), our family will sometimes say the "Bless us, oh Lord" prayer, but at other times, one of the prayer leaders (the kids) will "make one up." I especially love those. God has been thanked for inventing tacos, helping so-and-so pee in the potty, and even for Mom burning the food so we had to order pizza. This prayer before meals has become as commonplace as asking someone to pass the salt, and it's even gone from the confines of our humble abode into the restaurants we frequent.

TAKE STOCK

When did we last pray together as a family?
_____ When is our next family prayer time
scheduled?_____

What's something I can do to really make our family
prayer special?_____

Have I made praying with my spouse a top priority?
☐ Yes or ☐ No

Staying Catholic throughout the year — I'm a planner. You
know, a "to-do list" kind of guy. I'm this way because I
have to be. I've got far too many plates spinning and I
don't want any crashing to the ground. I know that I'm not
the only one on this planet who's striving to "get it all
done." This is why corporations have strategic planning
meetings, and bookstores sell a countless supply of day
planners and how-to books on time management. Next to
the very laptop I am typing on sits a dust-covered book
that promises to reveal the true secrets to personal and
family organization. The problem is, I just can't find the
time to read it.

The beauty about being a Catholic is that you can
scratch "plan special Catholic occasions" off your "to-do
list." It's done for ya. I just love it! Take a look at a

Catholic calendar and you'll see that the entire year is filled with rich liturgical seasons. You'll also notice feast days and holy days of obligation. It's like a well-thought-out spiritual roadmap designed to keep you from getting lost as you travel through the days, weeks, and months of your life.

❖ Feast Days

As my wife and I anticipated the baptism of our children — which is essentially claiming them for Christ — we thought it would be great to name each one after a holy man or woman. The Catholic Church has always lifted up men and women who have lived virtue-heroic lives (i.e., Mother Teresa). These saints don't usurp the role of Jesus, but serve as models of how we can live out our faith in Him.

In Chapter 4, I shared about how we celebrate a child's feast day in a similar fashion to his birthday — it truly is a day of honor and celebration. The birthday embraces the beginning of our child's life, and the feast day reminds us all that this life is temporary and that Jesus has prepared a place for each of us in His eternal home. Each child's saint becomes not only a heavenly mentor, if you will, but also a powerful prayer warrior for that child before the throne of God.

If you've never celebrated a feast day for yourself, or for your child, well, there's no time like the present. Grab a book on Catholic saints, or get typin' on your search engine. You'll be amazed at the incredibly diverse selection of virtuous men and women who make up our greater Catholic family. My wife, Colleen, had a terrible time finding a saint or biblical reference with her name. So she spent some time researching holy women and was touched to the core by the fervent prayer life of St. Monica (the mother who prayed without ceasing for the conversion of not only her husband, but also her now-famous son, St. Augustine). You can also dive into Scripture and select a biblical hero that you'd like to emulate. Have some fun with it!

❖ Liturgical Seasons

Advent is one such season set apart by the Church. It's a four-week period of time with the sole (pun intended) purpose of preparing our hearts to celebrate Christmas. During Advent, our family erects a plain evergreen tree, and each night we decorate it with a handmade Jesse Tree ornament. Each one depicts a part of the story of our salvation, from Creation all the way to the birth of Christ. With each felt ornament placed on the tree, our children grow more and more excited. On Christmas Eve, we blast the Christmas carols and decorate the tree with colored lights and more ornaments. The waiting is over, and it's time to rejoice in the birth of the Babe Who rests peacefully in the manger.

Lent is another season that helps to keep us focused. During these forty days, our family life is chock-full of spiritual practices that invite prayerfulness and discipline. It's a time to prepare our hearts to celebrate the Lord's glorious resurrection by remembering that He suffered and died on the cross for our sins.

The centerpiece at our Lenten dinner table is a crown of thorns, a braided loaf of bread in the shape of a circle, with toothpicks sticking out from it in all directions. This is a visual reminder that our sins contributed to Christ's sufferings. At the end of the meal, each child

ROLL UP YOUR SLEEVES RESOURCES

- *Voices of the Saints: A 365-Day Journey With Our Spiritual Companions,* by Bert Ghezzi
- *Book of Saints,* by Amy Welborn
- *Around the Year with the Trapp Family,* by Maria von Trapp
- *The Domestic Church: Room by Room,* by Donna Marie Cooper O'Boyle

is allowed to remove a "thorn" for every charitable act or special prayer said that day. In this way, we can share in the Passion, and realize that though He suffered for our sins, each kindness or offering we make actually lessened that suffering.

Most Catholics talk about their Lenten resolutions, which are comprised of acts of charity, special times of prayer, and things they wish to abstain from (i.e., chocolate, watching TV, etc.). Listen, it might be easy to "just say no" to chocolate for a day, but for someone like my wife (sorry to throw you under the bus, honey) to give up chocolate for forty days — well, we're now entering heroic virtue territory. What's key here is that our Lenten resolutions bring us closer to Christ and what He did for us. He is Love incarnate, and He laid down his life for all of mankind. Can you think of a better definition of charity? He was the Son of God, and yet spent considerable time in prayer. And nobody sacrificed or gave up more than Christ did for you and me.

Lent is a terrific time to make sure our spiritual muscles aren't getting flabby. To emphasize the importance of our resolutions, I actually like to buy a piece of poster board from the local drugstore. On it, each family member will list the spiritual practices to be embraced over the next forty days. Some will list items they'll give up, like candy or soda pop. Others may list that they will endeavor to pray more by reading the scriptures on a daily basis. You get the point.

We have found tremendous benefit in sharing personal spiritual goals with others in the family. The subtle message is deposited in each kid's mind that we're in this together. We're going to worship Him together. Serve Him together. Seek His forgiveness together. Live for Him together. And, God willing, be together again in Heaven when we pass from this world to the next.

TAKE STOCK

Have I introduced my kids to the awesome Catholic figures who have gone before us? ☐ Yes or ☐ No

Do I have the feast day of my spouse and kids circled on the calendar? ☐ Yes or ☐ No

Do I embrace the different seasons of the Church and do unique things with my kids so that they can understand and celebrate these periods of time?
☐ Yes or ☐ No

What are some very practical things I can do right now so that my family lives out our faith throughout the year?

_____

_____

Well, my oatmeal is just about gone, and I'm ready for a refill on my coffee. But before I go, please allow me to thank you for taking the time to join me for a spell. I thought it was important to provide a quick insight from the vantage point of sittin' in a Catholic pew. Oh, there's so much more that can be said, I know (about these topics and others), but it's really time to place this book on the shelf, roll up our sleeves, and get to work.

The truth is, I never set out to write an encyclopedic

volume covering parenting topics A-Z. This book is meant to serve as a starting point for someone who feels overwhelmed, lost, or a little bit stale in their parenting (time to throw that unwanted cereal box away).

My redheaded four-year-old, Danny, needs to use our white plastic stool if he wants to wash his hands at the sink. This $3.99 item allows him to go to a place he otherwise would be unable to get to. Hopefully this book is more valuable than a cheap stool, but it's supposed to serve the same end — to help you "step up" to a higher level of faith-filled parenting — *parenting on purpose!*

About the Author

Jason Free is a dynamic communicator, known for his unique blend of humor, wisdom, and straightforward style. Audiences connect with his personal stories and inspirational insights as Jason spurs them on to take their life and faith to the next level. He holds a bachelor's degree in philosophy and a master's degree in social work with a specialization in family therapy. Jason has served as director of a rural soup kitchen, substance abuse counselor, adjunct professor at the graduate level, general manager of the National Shrine of The Divine Mercy and currently as an entrepreneur in the financial services field. An avid sports fan and mentor, Jason is a favorite little league baseball coach and Boy Scout leader, and all around expert at planning unforgettable adventures! He and his wife, Colleen, have been married for seventeen years and are the proud parents of 8 children.

Colleen Free is a devoted wife, Catholic blogger, and homeschooling mother of 8 children, putting her degree in Elementary Education to good use on the home front.

A former writer and editor for the *Marian Helper* magazine, she has also provided editorial assistance for MercySong Ministries of Healing and is the author of *Praying with St. Faustina* (Marian Press). Colleen is also a professional singer with a beautiful soprano voice. She is featured on many of the Flynn family music albums, available through Mercysong, and she and Jason recite the rosary on three of MercySong's devotional CDs. A frequent soloist for weddings and funerals, she is one of the lead singers on the original Chaplet of Divine Mercy (shown on International television every weekday) and has spoken and sung at various events around the country, both with her husband and with MercySong. She is the eldest daughter of best-selling author and speaker Vinny Flynn.